REFLECTIONS

OF A COUNTRY
D·O·C·T·O·R

REFLECTIONS

OF A COUNTRY
D·O·C·T·O·R

BARRY LADD, M.D.

Glenbridge Publishing Ltd.

Library of Congress Catalog Card Number: LC 95-77536

International Standard Book Number: 0-944435-37-8

Printed in the U.S.A.

This book is dedicated to the patients whose confidence and trust in me gave me my life's work

and

To all the family physicians who continue to be dedicated to their patients and their profession

CONTENTS

OUR TOWN

I need to introduce myself. My name is Barry Ladd. I am a family physician. I practiced medicine for thirty years in a small country town, forty miles south of Chicago. I have always called it "Our Town" because the residents, including myself, so personally identified with the community.

We were quite rural. The people were mostly farmers and mill hands who worked in nearby industry. Until recently, we were relatively isolated due to minimal public transportation.

Our population grew by reproduction rather than by immigration. The typical pattern was to marry your high school sweetheart, move to a house three blocks from mama and make babies. These children, in turn, grew up and repeated the cycle. You could never talk about anybody, because sooner or later they were related by marriage.

In the thirty years I practiced in Our Town, I delivered fifteen hundred babies and had one hundred and eighty thousand office visits. I delivered the babies of the babies, and took care of four generations in the same family.

During that time, there was an explosion of technology and scientific information. The practice of medicine shifted from being more of an art to being more of a science. Physicians routinely do things today that would have been considered miraculous thirty years ago. We are all physically better for it. Life expectancy at birth went from seventy years in 1963 to seventy-six years in 1993. Diseases that were painfully progressive, many of them fatal, are quite treatable today. People suffer less and live longer.

During this time, I was a participant and an observer. I saw how personal events and decisions played out over time. I want to tell you what I saw, heard, and felt. These are all true stories. Some are composites of several people. In some of the stories, I have taken the liberty of expressing what I felt the patients' thoughts were. I have changed the names in order to protect the privacy of the individuals and families involved. The family names used are made up to reflect the ethnic composition of Our Town.

Come, make rounds with me. Please be quiet, you are an observer!

FIRST DAY

It was a momentous day. It was a major milestone in my life. After all the years of training, preparing, dreaming and planning, I was finally on my own. I was ready, looking forward to saving lives and stamping out disease. I had joined a small group of family doctors in "Our Town," and this was my first day in private practice. It was actually the first day of the rest of my life. The feeling was awesome!

I started the day at the clinic, and as soon as I walked in the door, Emma turned me around and sent me out on an emergency house call with a town map in one hand and my shiny black bag in the other. I found the address with no difficulty, rang the bell, and was ushered in with the whisper, "He's upstairs."

Paul Marcus sat on the edge of the bed leaning forward. His skin was pasty gray, covered with sweat and cold to the touch. He did not know me and really didn't care who I was. He simply said, "This one is much worse than last time. My chest is killing me." His wife touched my arm and said, "He had a heart attack four months ago and takes nitroglycerin, but it isn't helping today." I opened my bag and reached for the morphine, but I never got to use it.

Paul pitched forward onto the floor. He fell on his face, and his glasses flew off. One lens popped out of the frame and spun crazily on the floor. His wife and I were momentarily terrorized, and I forced myself to take control. I told her to get on the phone and get help. Then, I threw myself on the floor to try to resuscitate Mr. Marcus.

I felt for a pulse in his neck. There was none. I rolled him over on his back and slammed my fist, hard, in the center of his chest to no avail. I swept my fingers through his mouth, removed his false teeth and slipped in a plastic airway. I blew his lungs up with three quick puffs and set the rhythm of resuscitation with five chest compressions, followed by one lung inflation, followed by five chest compressions, and so on and on and on. I set the rhythm and I couldn't stop. His heart rate and breathing became my only focus, and I was oblivious to everything else around me. I lost track of time. I saw nothing. I heard nothing. I just kept pumping and puffing. I couldn't stop.

Finally, I felt a pair of gentle hands take hold of mine and heard a soft voice telling me that I should stop. "Paul is dead. Nothing will bring him back." I said, "Impossible! I have him under control." A firmer, in charge voice said, "His pupils are fixed and dilated. You must stop." I looked up and the room was full of people. Paul's wife was sobbing and holding on to a police officer. Her tears spotted his shirt. Kneeling opposite me, on the other side of Paul's body was a distinguished gray-haired physician who later became my mentor. He held me and, over Paul's dead body, quietly told me, "Your job is to do everything you can to help your patient, but all of them die eventually. There is no way of avoiding or preventing it. It's not your fault. You did your best. Today is Paul's day to die. Tomorrow it may be mine, and eventually it will be yours."

I hugged him tightly and thanked him. I stuffed all my tools in the shiny bag. I expressed my sympathy to the family and made my way back to the car. I sat there holding on to the steering wheel. Tears streamed down my face and dripped off the sides of my chin. It was so hard to accept. It took an hour before I could regain my composure and return to the office.

All this happened more than thirty years ago. I don't know how many death certificates I have signed. I can never do it without thinking that today it's him, tomorrow it's someone else, and eventually it will be me.

GRANNY

Carl was sixty years old and lived with his mother. She was not his "angel mother" and he did not stay with her to take care of her. It was the opposite. Carl was what is generally referred to as "slow." He could manage all right as long as someone supervised him and watched out for him.

They lived on a large farm that Granny's grandparents had homesteaded. Carl was pleasant and good-natured. He was a hard worker and, under her guidance, the farm prospered. Folks, being the way they are, speculated on what would happen to Carl and the farm when the old lady passed on. (Today it is a huge shopping mall.)

Over the years, Carl had his share of women at the house, but none of them wanted to marry and neither did he. The women didn't want the package of Carl and Granny; so Carl had the best of both worlds.

Carl called the office one morning and asked me to come out to the farm because he couldn't wake his mother up. I assumed she had a stroke.

As I drove through the countryside, I reviewed her history in my mind. She was eighty-five and had raised four children. Carl was the youngest. She had insulin-dependent diabetes and managed it quite well. She watched her diet and took forty units of NPH insulin every morning. She had no complications from diabetes in the past. She was on no other medication.

I thought about the woman herself. Her husband had been killed in a farming accident twenty years ago. She was tough and hard working. It was people like her, endowed with the work ethic and the pioneer spirit, that had made America great. She and her family had farmed six hundred acres of Illinois prairie at a time when it was done with horses and mules. During the hard work season, she fed a dozen hired hands three huge meals a day without a microwave or a dishwasher. This woman was living Americana, and it seemed that it was coming to an end.

I pulled into the barnyard and was greeted by a snarling German shepherd dog. His hackles were up, and his front paws were on the driver's side window. I sat in the car and waited for Carl to come out and get the dog, but nothing happened. I honked the horn and the upstairs window opened. Carl yelled down to me that the dog was perfectly safe. I yelled back, "I'm not concerned about the dog's safety! If you want me to see your mother, you'd better come down and chain him up." He came out laughing and teasing as he tied up the dog.

Granny was in the upstairs bedroom, "A rag, a bone, and a hank of hair." She appeared to be in a coma. She was no longer the image of strength. Her temperature was 103 and her pulse was rapid and thready. She was terribly short of breath, and there was the smell of acetone in the room. Her mouth was open and dry.

Further examination revealed that Granny had pneumonia. I turned to Carl and told him that his mother was dying and that I would make arrangements to admit her to the hospital. I assured him that I would do whatever I could to help her. He replied, "Ma always told me she didn't want to go to no hospital. If she's going to die, she might as well die in her own bed." I told him that I could treat her better at the hospital, and that she might recover there. He said, "No. Whatever you are going to do, do here." In a way he was right. Her chances of surviving ranged from slim to none.

In those days the black bag had everything. We didn't have paramedics, and so the black bag brought as much of the hospital to the patient as the doctor could reasonably carry. The physician's skill, plus the contents of the black bag, enabled patients to be treated at home. Today, home health agencies all over the country are providing the same service.

I started an IV with a bottle of saline and added bicarbonate and five million units of rapid-acting penicillin to it. Lanoxin for her heart flowed through the thin plastic tubing along with large doses of rapid-acting regular insulin. Long-acting insulin and penicillin were injected into her emaciated muscles. Carl watched silently as the last of the fluids flowed into her veins and the IV was disconnected.

As I left, I said, "Call me if anything happens." He said he would, and then asked, "What should I feed her when she wakes up?" I started to tell him that I doubted that she would wake up, but I softened the blow with, "When she wakes up, give her some iced tea with lots of sugar in it."

Back at the office, it was like a vigil waiting for Carl to call. The afternoon moved to evening with no call. I had so much work to do that I didn't have time to go back. There was nothing more that I could do anyway. The next morning my nurse Barbara answered the phone. She turned to me and said, "Carl wants to talk to you." I picked up the phone and said in my most compassionate tone, "How's it going Carl." He replied, "Not good, Granny is tearing up the house. She told me to tell you she's sick to death of that damned ice tea, and if she can't get anything else to eat, she's going to get a new doctor."

When Granny was ninety-two she had her appendix removed. At ninety-five, she passed away quietly at home.

After Granny died, Carl sold the farm to a developer, took the money, went to Florida, and I never heard from him again.

IT'S TIME

By the time I entered private practice, home deliveries were rarely done. However, during my career, I had several home deliveries. I hadn't planned any of them. It just worked out that way.

I had been in practice for about a year when the phone rang in the middle of the night and an unfamiliar voice said, "It's time." I didn't have a clue who I was talking to, and my natural reply was, "Time for what?" Frank Ludwig, a local pig farmer, answered, "Baby's coming."

I jumped out of bed, grabbed the black bag, and was on my way. I didn't know these people, but I did know an adventure was coming.

The farm was far out in the country. The old house stood at the junction between two unmarked, unlit gravel roads. It was pitch black with no ambient light, just myriads of stars decorating the sky. It was perfectly quiet. Not even a barking dog. I felt totally isolated, and it seemed as if I had gone back in time.

Frank answered the door, and we introduced ourselves. He said he appreciated my coming out. He was

10

terrified of the prospect of having to deliver the baby. He had delivered the last one. It had been such a bloody mess, and he was not going to do that again.

This was Mrs. Ludwig's fifth pregnancy. Although her first two babies were delivered in a hospital, she was absolutely phobic about them and refused to go to one again for any reason. Her third baby was delivered at home by a local doctor who had since left the area. Frank had delivered the last baby. After all, "If you can deliver piglets, you can certainly deliver one of your own children." So here I was with a woman in labor, who was absolutely terrified she would be taken to the hospital, and a husband who was equally terrified she wouldn't.

I attempted to be a voice of reason in a small world in chaos. I explained to her that I would not take her to the hospital unless a great life-threatening situation developed. I explained to Frank that women have been having babies for hundreds of thousands of years and that they obviously do it well. It has only been in the past fifty years that hospitals have been used for routine childbirth. I further reassured him that, since she had delivered four times before without a complication, she should do fine now. He replied, "It's in your hands, Doc, I'm going to get drunk." I said, "No! You're going to boil water, and if you can't help, get me somebody who can." I don't know why I said that. I didn't need any boiling water, but that's what they say in all the old western movies.

I broke her bag of water and her labor progressed rapidly. She was an excellent patient and had great self-control. In three hours, we delivered a healthy boy with no complications, no stitches, and minimal bleeding. At the door, Frank thanked me and asked, "How much do I owe you?" I told him, "Seventy-five dollars." He went to the cupboard, opened a coffee can, and paid in cash.

The sun was just coming up when I left the gravel road. I returned to the blacktop and the twentieth century.

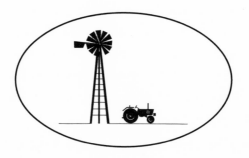

ISOBELLA

A physician is thought of as a helping person. He has a special expertise that enables him to help in a precise manner. A clergyman, a nurse, and a best friend are also helping persons. They too have a special expertise to help in a precise manner.

Physicians are healers and think in terms of curing the patient, but all patients eventually die. When the patient has an incurable disease, the healer can no longer think in terms of cure, but only in terms of comfort. He then, hopefully, becomes more like the clergyman, the nurse, or the best friend.

I have always felt that there was a contract that bound me to my patient. It was unspoken, but it was like an exchange of vows. The patient knows that I am his personal physician. He will bring me all his problems because he knows I will try to help him. I, in turn, know that this is my patient, and I will do everything I can to help him, until death do us part.

Our Town is a Catholic community. Although only five thousand people live here, we have three Catholic parishes, a seminary, a monastery, a Catholic girls' high school, and the mother house of a large convent.

Sister Isobella sat in my office, shrouded in a total mass of black from which peered out a very pale face with bright eyes. She said she didn't feel good and had been very tired for several months. She had not lost any weight, but thought that she might be running fevers because sometimes she would have terrible sweats at night. Within the last week, several swellings had appeared in her neck, and she knew they had not been there before.

Physical examination suggested the worst. She had enlarged lymph glands in her neck and armpit, and an enlarged liver and spleen. I hoped that she had "mono," a common infection in young people. Laboratory testing and biopsy confirmed advanced lymphoma, a malignancy that in 1963 was always fatal. There was no specific therapy that would even prolong her life. How could I tell this girl of twenty-three that she was dying?

Mother Superior, Sister Isobella, and I sat in a small room close to one another. I carefully explained the diagnosis and the natural course of her disease. I told them that there was no treatment that would cure her or prolong her life. Disciplined disciples that they were, they accepted this information with equanimity. Sister Isobella asked, "Is there anything you can do to make me feel better?" I said, "Yes, I can." Her resolve to be strong wavered just a bit. Her fear surfaced when she said, "Please don't let me suffer." I assured her, "I wouldn't." "Would you like another opinion from Loyola University Medical Center?" I asked. The reply was a simple "No."

A dying person makes no long-range plans. As they approach death, their time frames become shorter. It's no longer planning for next year, but planning for next month, then next week, and eventually one day at a time. The family physician should be there for comfort and support until the very last day.

She began palliative chemotherapy with drugs, which are no longer in use. She felt better and her strength returned. The swellings went away. Once in remission, she came to the office monthly to have the state of her disease evaluated by her symptoms and physical findings. We talked about all kinds of things including growing up on a farm in Ohio and how she was called to the religious life. Within six months her disease had recurred.

As the lymphoma began to involve other organ systems, she became quite debilitated. She couldn't come to the clinic anymore and moved into the convent infirmary where the sisters could take care of her. I continued to treat her with the goal being that of comfort. I gave her blood transfusions and oxygen to improve her breathing. I prescribed medications to keep her free of pain. She finally asked that I stop treatment, saying that she was at peace with herself and was not afraid. We comforted each other. I had not realized how attached I had become to her.

I continued to visit each day just to sit and talk, never opening the black bag, never examining her. Each time I left her I said, "I will see you again tomorrow." On the very last day she replied, "I will not be here. I will be with my Father."

I never saw her again, and I have never quite recovered. I cannot think of those days without a profound feeling of sadness.

HAVE A NICE DAY

For a long, long time the standard salutations in America were, "good morning," "good afternoon," "good evening," and "good night." Sometimes it was, "how are you." But today the preferred salutation is, "have a nice day."

I recently said that to a person who constantly works with people, and she replied, "It's hard to have a nice day when you deal with the public." The public is us. Why are we so difficult to deal with? I have thought about it for a while, and I think I have the answer.

Three percent of the population suffer from psychosis. Psychosis is defined as a profound disorganization of the mind, personality, or behavior, which results from the individual's inability to tolerate the demands of his social environment. Their logic and thought processes are defective, and these people are thought of as "crazy."

Six percent of the population are chronically depressed. They are unhappy people and are on a perpetual "downer." They are hard to live with and hard to be around.

Ten percent of the population have problems with substance abuse. They are alcoholics or drug users.

Another ten percent have chronic anxiety. They are nervous and irritable people.

Add to this the large number of people physically suffering the effects of organic, debilitating diseases such as arthritis, heart failure, emphysema, cancer, etc., and it's no wonder the public is hard to deal with!

If you deal with the public and relate to one hundred people in a day, at least one third of them are disturbed and distressed in one way or another. That's one out of three. Whenever you have a confrontation with such a person, you must consider if it's your fault. If it is, you must correct your position and make it right. If it is not, you should do everything reasonable to help such a person as they already have a considerable burden to bear!

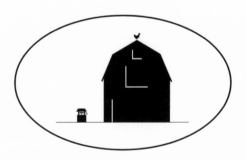

THE MAN WITH
THE YELLOW EYES

Frankenstein is alive and well and resides in Our Town. I know, because he comes to my office once a month.

I first met him in 1985. He was an imposing and frightening figure even at seventy-five years of age. He stood six feet, four inches tall and weighed two hundred and sixty-five pounds. He had a neurological disorder that caused his arms and legs to be in constant motion with twitches, jerks, and spasms. His speech was punctuated with the same disorder. His voice was deep and gravelly, like a growl. His gait was wide-based and lurching. There was an ever-present cigarette in his left hand, which glowed red when his arm flailed about and occasionally made it to his mouth for a short, fast, urgent puff. His teeth were snags; one gold, the others yellowed and stained with sixty years of cigarette tar. His eyes were bright yellow and luminescent compared to his dull yellow skin. When he lurched into my crowded waiting room and sat down

19

heavily in the closest chair, six other patients moved as far from him as possible!

In the examining room he proved to be an intelligent man and an excellent observer. With great effort, in distorted bursts of words that were formed clearly in his mind, he told me of his illness. He said that he had been in good health all of his life and had never had a significant illness. He had experienced mild tremors for as long as he could remember, but they had worsened over the past twenty years, and he had been unable to work for the past ten. He was so used to them that he considered them only an inconvenience. He came to see me because for the past month his urine resembled Coca Cola and his skin was dry, itchy, and turning yellowish green. In the past week the whites of his eyes had become bright yellow, and he was a little nauseated.

His physical examination revealed several medical problems, the most serious being the jaundice and enlarged liver. I explained to him the possible causes of his illness and recommended he be hospitalized for testing and treatment. His one word answer was, "No."

Old folks usually try their best to stay out of hospitals because, in their experience, hospitals were places where people went to die. I told him that he needed to be in a hospital, and he told me he could not go because he was responsible for his disabled sister. I assured him that we could make some arrangement to take care of her, and tried to impress upon him the need for further tests and treatment. The discussion ended with him saying that there was no one to care for his sister. With that, he stood up and lurched out of the clinic.

I was bewildered and fascinated. Who was this strange man and what was his story? How could he care for someone else when it appeared that he could barely take care of himself? He had walked to the clinic, a distance of four blocks, and was now walking home to a run-down house in an old neighborhood.

That evening I visited a friend of mine in that neighborhood. He told the story of a man who for the past fifty years had provided a home and a life for his sister. He had never married and had worked as a farmer, laborer, and odd-job man to provide for himself and his sister since the death of their parents. This happened when he was a young man and his sister was a teenager. She was severely disabled and mentally retarded. She had great difficulty speaking, and had the same familial tremor as her brother. In years past, she had been quiet and would sit for hours in one place waiting for him to return from work. In recent years she had become more agitated, and would shriek and cry out unintelligibly at all hours. I could not imagine how he, with all his afflictions, could feed, bathe, and clothe her. But he did; and he did it well. Because he spent so much time at home, he developed homemaker skills. He learned to cook and bake. He distributed home-baked bread and cookies throughout the neighborhood. (Would you take a cookie from such a man?)

In most neighborhoods, such a couple would be shunned by adults and tormented by teenagers. But just as he had assumed responsibility for his sister, the neighborhood assumed responsibility for them both. Teenagers cut the grass in summer and shoveled the snow in winter. Adults, on the way to the supermarket, stopped and asked if he needed anything from the store. It had been this way for almost twenty years. Anyone who spoke of him always added the phrase, "And he's such a nice man, once you get to know him."

I stopped at the house and spoke with him again about being admitted to the hospital. I pointed out that without treatment he might die leaving no one to care for his sister. He finally agreed that he would go, if I found someone to care for her.

I didn't have to do a thing. The next day a lady from Wisconsin called to tell me that she would arrive on Saturday and would be able to handle the sister. She had grown up in the neighborhood, married, and moved to Wisconsin. When she heard about the problem, she decided to come and help "the cookie monster."

The man with the yellow eyes was admitted. The diagnosis turned out to be an obstructing gallstone, which was removed along with his gallbladder. There were no post-operative complications, and he made a complete recovery. Nurses, doctors, and other patients all agreed, "He's such a nice man, once you get to know him."

His sister died about two years later leaving him free, but alone.

Last week I went to a grade school graduation party. He was there as a guest and contributed to the party by bringing his concertina. He was taking requests. But it didn't make any difference what you requested; he always played the same piece. It was the only one he could play! He played music the same way he walked and talked, with lurches, twitches, and tremors! Guests from outside the neighborhood asked about him and were told, "He's such a nice man, once you get to know him."

CHEMISTRY

When you meet someone and are immediately attracted to that person, it is called good vibrations. Good vibrations are easy to deal with. These people usually become your friends or associates or just pleasant acquaintances. It is not a sexual thing. However, every now and then you will meet someone for whom you will have an unbelievable, immediate, and almost uncontrollable sexual attraction. There is no explanation for it. It's not "love at first sight," but more likely "lust at first sight." The advice for a married man is to avoid it. Run away and don't look back. It will destroy you if you don't. If you are single when this happens, I guess the advice would be, "go for it!"

In my medical career, I have had one hundred and eighty thousand patient visits. I would estimate that one hundred thousand of those visits were adult women. This phenomenon of attraction has happened to me just three times. I have talked with many doctors in my age group, and most of them admit to the same experience, including one doctor who did not run away and was almost destroyed.

Let me tell you of my last episode. It happened ten years ago.

I was on obstetrics and gynecology board call for the hospital emergency room. About ten o'clock in the evening the emergency room called me to see a patient with heavy vaginal bleeding. The patient was a thirty-year-old married woman who was driving by herself from Detroit to St. Louis to visit her mother. As she drove through the Chicago area, she began bleeding and cramping. She assumed that her period, which was late, was starting. But the bleeding and cramping became unusually severe, and when she saw the sign on the highway indicating the location of a hospital, she exited and presented herself to the emergency room.

As soon as I walked into the room, I knew she was one of those events. I thought she was the most beautiful, sensuous woman in the world. Her voice was mesmerizing. There was a delicious smell about her. I could hardly concentrate on taking a history. I broke out in a sweat and had palpitations. It was most unnerving as I had a tremor in my hands and in my voice.

The patient's diagnosis was an incomplete miscarriage. The treatment was a D and C, which I performed at midnight and promptly went home.

At seven o'clock in the morning I called my partner and told him what had happened. I asked him to see the patient for me, and if all was well, send her home. I certainly could not and would not see her. If she asked me to drive her to St. Louis, I probably would have!

I saw my partner later that afternoon. He said, "You know, you really are crazy. She's just an ordinary everyday average person."

EFFICIENCY

My mentor was a marvel of efficiency and practicality. He had practiced at a time when medical supplies were not prepackaged, sterile, or disposable. Injection syringes were made of glass and had to be sterilized after each use. Needles were sharpened, sterilized, and used again and again. The same was true of scalpel blades, but he complained that once they were dull, he could never get them sharp enough again. So, in the office, for anything that needed an incision, he used Gillette double-edged razor blades. (Gillette never knew it was in the scalpel business and was the first in prepackaged, throwaway medical supplies!) With the aid of two hemostats, one straight and one curved, he could snap a razor blade into any shape or size that he desired.

I had just started in practice when a patient came in with a "felon," which is a deep abscess of the tendon sheath of a finger. It is extremely painful!

I knew what it was and what I was supposed to do with it, but I had never actually seen or treated one before.

I asked my mentor to look at it and treat it for me. The proper treatment is to make a deep incision on both sides of the finger to drain out the pus. A rubber tube is then pushed through the incisions to stick out on both sides, which prevents the abscess from forming again.

He unwrapped a double-edged razor blade and snapped it into a long pointy blade. Before the patient could say "sonofabitch," he had slashed both sides of the finger relieving the pain and pressure as copious amounts of pus poured out. He then peeled off his rubber gloves, cut off one rubber finger, and poked it through the incision as a rubber drain. The whole procedure took less than sixty seconds.

The patient and I were greatly relieved when it was over!

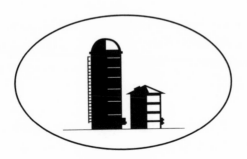

NO LUCK

The rapid ringing of the emergency entrance bell reflected the panic of the patient's wife as she pushed the button again and again. Her anxiety was transmitted to us as we responded to the sound and carried old Mr. Cravalish from his car to the emergency room table.

It was ten o'clock in the morning. Henry and his wife were driving to town for groceries when the chest pain started. At first the squeezing pain would come and go and felt like indigestion. Henry silently resolved to give up the breakfast bacon and eggs, which had been a lifetime habit. Then the pain came and stayed. It was squeezing across his chest, and he could hardly breathe. It radiated up into his neck, and he began to sweat profusely. He was lightheaded and felt as if he were going to pass out. He thought to himself, "I must be dying," and told his wife, who was driving, to take him to the clinic.

Morphine was given. Oxygen was started. An intravenous line was inserted, and the electrocardiogram connected. His blood pressure was low, but adequate. The cardiac tracing showed an acute myocardial infarction. Henry was comfortable and quiet. His wife was not. She kept repeating, "I have no luck. My first two husbands died the same way. I have no luck."

Henry appeared to be stable. We called the paramedics to transfer him to the local hospital. As they moved him from the table to the litter, his heart rhythm became abnormal and rapidly progressed to a dangerous rate. "I have no luck." Intravenous drugs were given and the rhythm corrected temporarily. His blood pressure fell, and he became unconscious. The arrhythmia was now life threatening. "I have no luck." We shocked him with electric paddles and the rhythm became normal but quickly deteriorated again. "I have no luck." We shocked him again and the rhythm became a flat line.

"No luck, no luck at all."

SERENDIPITY

I have often seen illustrations depicting guardian angels in roadside gift shops across America. They are usually prints showing innocent children in grave danger. They are generally done in a natural setting such as a woods, a river, or a cliff. There is always a winged female figure in the background protecting or guiding them.

Do we really have guardian angels or is it serendipity? Does the Lord work in strange and mysterious ways, or do some people just get lucky? I want to tell you about three cases from my practice and let you decide.

Marsha

Marsha Purdy was a very happy young woman. Her husband, Ron, adored her, and she thought he was the best thing that ever happened to her. They had two healthy children, one in kindergarten and a two-year-old at home. Ron had a successful business and made good money. Marsha was a genuine homemaker who thrived in a role of providing a solid base of emotional and physical support for her family. Both Marsha and Ron had grown up in Our Town with their friends and family all around them. It was the American dream come true; a happy marriage, two kids, no money problems, many friends, and a loving extended family nearby.

Then it all changed. It started slowly. Marsha began having what she described as "spells." She would be her usual self and then for no obvious reason she would become anxious and nervous. She often had a feeling of impending disaster. She would sweat and shake, and her heart would pound. After an hour or so her symptoms would gradually subside, and she would be all right again. When she tried to discover a cause for her symptoms, she drew a blank. With the passage of time, the spells occurred more frequently and lasted longer. She lost weight and had trouble sleeping. She worried constantly and began to think she was losing her mind.

I had been her doctor for most of her life. I had delivered both of her children and felt that I knew her well. I considered her to be an emotionally stable person.

There is a saying in medicine that every neurotic eventually dies of a real disease. Therefore, every patient coming to me with emotional symptoms gets a complete medical evaluation. Marsha was no exception. Her detailed medical history suggested several organic diseases from the common to the rare, as well as some psychiatric diagnoses. Her physical examination was normal except for a small black scaly spot, highly suggestive of melanoma, in the middle of her back.

I was concerned about the possibility that this highly malignant skin cancer might have spread to her brain and was the cause of her emotional instability. I did not add to her fears by discussing the possibilities, but simply explained that she needed further studies. Her brain scan and EEG were normal as were a myriad of other tests, which ruled out organic disease.

The skin growth was still a significant problem, and it was removed. The pathologist confirmed that it was a malignant melanoma. Fortunately, there was no evidence that this potentially lethal skin cancer had spread.

Within a week her spells disappeared completely and have never returned. It has been six years since the melanoma was removed, and there has been no recurrence or evidence that it had spread.

There was absolutely no relationship between the melanoma and her emotional symptoms except that the spells brought her to my office. If she had not come, the melanoma probably would have gone undetected and she would be dead. You explain it. Was it a guardian angel that guided her to my office or was it serendipity?

Richard

Richard Hardy was a successful businessman. He was a senior executive with a large company in our area. Like most men in his position, he was married to his job. He spent most of his waking hours at the office and had the job on his mind when he did get home. He was also married to Ruth.

It was very hard to be married to them both, job and wife. He felt that he was a good husband and father. He was certainly a terrific breadwinner. The family had social status, a beautiful home, education, and all of the good life that money could provide. Ruth, on the other hand, wanted more. She wanted him. She felt that, as a team, they had done well. She was responsible for hearth and home. He was responsible for income. The children were grown and gone, and Richard and Ruth certainly had enough money to live comfortably. She wanted him to retire so that they could do all the things that they missed out on when the children were growing up.

Richard truly loved Ruth and wanted the same things, but his other wife, the job, also made her demands known. He was an intensely loyal, responsible man. Unfortunately, he had two wives, and he couldn't please them both.

As a successful businessman, Richard was good at negotiation and compromise, and he soon struck a deal. He was fifty-seven years old and decided that he would retire at sixty-two. This seemed reasonable to both his wife and his company.

"Man plans and God laughs."

Richard did not retire at sixty-two. He retired at fifty-nine when Ruth developed Alzheimer's disease. It gradually progressed to where Richard could no longer take care of her. He put her in a nursing home and returned to his empty house. Burdened with guilt, his home became his prison.

After some time had passed, his married son came from California to check on him. He found his father in a deep depression, and he brought him to me.

This was not the Richard Hardy I had known. My Richard Hardy was a powerful, "in charge" man who employed several hundred people. The man who came to see me appeared small, weak, and helpless. He stared at the floor as if studying the patterns. He looked up startled and bewildered when I addressed him by name.

We talked and he told me what a terrible failure he was. He failed his wife, failed his company, and there was no hope for him. He would just as soon die as go on living this way. I asked him if he really wanted to die, and he assured me he did.

I admitted him to the psychiatric unit of the hospital under the care of a psychiatrist. I continued to see him frequently as he was my patient, and I was bound to him by the same loyalty that bound him to his company.

In those days, before we had the miraculous antidepressant drugs of today, electroshock produced the most rapid results. Richard was given this treatment and responded favorably. Three weeks later he was discharged from the hospital on medication. He saw his psychiatrist about once a week, and although he was considerably improved, his depression persisted.

About a month later, the police called and asked me to come to Mr. Hardy's house. Apparently, Richard had not been seen for several days, and worried neighbors called the police. When the police received no response to knocks on the door, they broke into the house and found him on the floor. He was unconscious, barely breathing, and cyanotic. Empty whisky and medicine bottles were all over the floor. He had taken all of his pills, plus whatever he had found in the medicine cabinet. It pretty much looked as if his suicide attempt would be successful.

At the hospital, he was maintained on a respirator and continuous intravenous fluids. On the third day he began to be more responsive. The respirator was discontinued, and he was able to breathe on his own, but remained in a coma. His neurological exam was diffusely abnormal. It was clear that his brain had been deprived of oxygen for a significant period of time.

A week later he opened his eyes and began to move his arms and legs. He was able to swallow and feed himself, but he did not speak. Two week later, I walked into the room and he said, "Good morning doctor," using a take-charge voice.

He recovered completely from the overdose. However, a lot of information had been erased from his brain. He had no memory of Ruth and very little memory of his job, except that he knew he had been good at it. He had a sense of humor and was delighted to know that he had money. The depression was gone!

If only we could get into the brain and erase selected emotionally charged material without damaging the rest. It would be like editing a tape or a movie, removing unwanted memories and images. I believe that is what happened to Mr. Hardy. But who was the editor? God's will or serendipity?

Jo Beth

Jo Beth Allison had a tough life. She was born with cerebral palsy, giving her a spastic right arm and leg. She was brought up in the Baptist Church, and her religious convictions gave her great comfort and strength. She married her childhood sweetheart in Tennessee, and they came to Our Town to find work. Ralph took a job at the steel mill, while she found work in a factory. Away from work, they were devoted to each other. You rarely saw one without the other.

Nature took it's course, and Jo Beth came to my office eight weeks pregnant. She was absolutely delighted with herself and referred to her pregnancy as a "gift from God." I, in turn, teased her and told her it was a "gift from Ralph."

In my office, complete obstetrical care averages about fifteen visits. During each visit, I evaluate the state and stage of the pregnancy. I talk about what is happening and what will happen as time goes by. Jo Beth and I talked about baby care and day-to-day personal problems. We became good friends in spite of her trying to make a Baptist out of me. I also talked about a Caesarean section because of her pelvic deformity, which was secondary to her cerebral palsy. She wasn't concerned and basically answered that the Lord would provide for her.

She reached term, her water ruptured, and she went into labor. Her labor progressed nicely. She dilated fairly rapidly, but the fetal head did not descend. She was fully dilated, but the head remained high and would not descend into her contracted pelvis. A C-section was performed, and she delivered a six-pound-five-ounce girl. Mother and child were doing fine!

As a new mother, she thrived. She breast-fed her child and gave up her job at the factory. She became a full-time wife and mother. Her spastic arm and leg were only an inconvenience.

Two years later she was pregnant again. In those days the rule of "once a C-section, always a C-section" prevailed, and at term, a repeat C-section produced another healthy girl. We had discussed tying Jo Beth's tubes with the repeat C-section to prevent future pregnancies. She and Ralph wanted that done as money was limited, and Jo Beth would have plenty of problems taking care of two babies. So, tubal ligation was done, and everyone went home happy.

I saw the baby at two weeks and all was well. Two weeks after that, the emergency room doctor at the hospital called to tell me that the baby had been found dead in her bassinet. He suggested that the cause of death was sudden infant death syndrome (SIDS). An autopsy revealed nothing.

I met with Jo Beth and Ralph to explain SIDS to them; they were devastated. How could the Lord have abandoned them. I was not much help, and they went home with their grief.

The next morning, one of my obstetrical colleagues called me. He had not heard about the death and did not know Jo Beth or Ralph. He called to tell me that he had delivered a healthy boy to an unwed mother who wanted to put him up for adoption. At that time, he had no infertile couple in his practice and wanted to know if I could place a baby with someone in my practice.

In thirty years of doing obstetrics, no one outside of my practice, other than that day, had ever offered me a baby for adoption. Jo Beth and Ralph adopted the baby and called him John, which means gift from God.

RIPPLES

It seems to me that when a good thing happens, it has a ripple effect. It makes other people feel good and inspires them to do good things.

I believe that evil also has a ripple effect. If we are surrounded by evil events, we become desensitized to its presence and accept it as the norm. Continuous exposure to violence in the media, either in the form of news reporting or as entertainment, desensitizes us to violence and allows it to perpetuate.

When bad things happen, it makes us feel bad, and our bodies, as well as our psyches, respond badly. In such an environment, a person with chronic depression may be "pushed over the edge" and take his own life. A person with a propensity for violence may get permission from the media to perpetrate it. There are many examples of life imitating art and copycat criminal events.

Richard Speck killed eight student nurses in 1966. That act of evil devastated eight specific families and affected thousands of others. I know for a fact that it caused the death of Stephanie Tregowski.

Stephanie was a widow who lived in Our Town. She was an excitable woman with high blood pressure. Her life revolved around her family, especially around her twenty-year-old granddaughter who was a nursing student in Chicago. It was three days after the murders that she came to my office. She was very anxious and tearful. She had been unable to eat or sleep since the murders and could not stop crying. Her granddaughter was all right, but she attended the same school and lived in the same neighborhood as the victims. "It could have been her," she wailed. As she talked about her feelings and her fears, she became more and more angry and agitated. She got up and paced around the room. She pounded on the desk and the walls. Her voice got louder and more shrill as she became more agitated and uncontrolled. I tried, unsuccessfully, to calm her and called the nurse to draw up a sedative to be given by injection.

She was red in the face, and in the middle of a sentence she stopped. It was quiet for two or three seconds before she collapsed to the floor. She was gasping for breath, and her body was twitching. We tried to resuscitate her to no avail. She had no pulse and no blood pressure. Her pupils became fixed and dilated.

Damn you to hell, Richard Speck!

THE PROFESSOR

The sign on the table at the Interstate Truck Stop read, "For Truckers Only." The tables were full of men wearing cowboy boots and flannel shirts. Their wallets were connected to their belts by long steel chains. Most of them wore billed caps emblazoned with company logos: Ruan, Red Ball Express, Navajo, Yellow Freight, etc. Some had team jackets to match. There was a constant rumble of conversation with dishes clanking in the background. One man at a table was not what he appeared to be. He wore a billed cap with "The Professor" embroidered on the front, and his team jacket proclaimed him to be a "Bears" fan. He had perfect white teeth, manicured nails, and a large diamond pinky ring. His plaid shirt was a "Pendleton." On the table were *The New York Times*, the *Farmers Almanac*, and a King James Bible. He was Clarence Cassity, conducting classes at the "Interstate."

I met him for the first time when he was seventy years old. He was already well-established at the truck stop and well-known all along the interstate highway system. He and his classes were often discussed over the CBs miles away from the truck stop.

He was the only child of an enormously wealthy family. Born at the turn of the century, he was raised in the isolated elegance of a Victorian mansion in Our Town. Initially, he was educated at home by a private tutor. But at thirteen, he was sent to a boarding school in New Hampshire. After graduating, he went to England and studied at Oxford. He was a true scholar in that he studied the things that interested and stimulated him without consideration for future employment or the need to make money. Clarence Cassity never had a paying job in his life. He was a sponge that sucked up information and held on to it. He studied Theology, History, Philosophy, and Ethics. He studied Biology and Mechanical Engineering. He read continuously and sought knowledge for its own sake. He was a living breathing encyclopedia. There were few subjects and little written that he didn't have some knowledge of. He was also psychologically "bent." He had never associated with ordinary people, and when he returned from school, the only people to greet him were his parents. He had no friends. To my knowledge, he had never dated, nor shown an interest in women. When his parents died, he lived and studied in the big mansion totally alone. All of this happened long before I met him.

Our Town was a small place with only one local restaurant. Clarence preferred not to eat there. Instead, he drove to Route 66 and ate at the truck stop. He would sit on the periphery of the action and observe. He watched and listened to the camaraderie of the truckers. He loved to hear the laughter and the baiting and banter of these coarse men. He secretly wished he could be one of them. He sat there in his English tweeds and no one paid the slightest attention to him.

I don't know how he finally broke into the truckers' club, but I suspect he spoke up to settle an argument. I have enjoyed dinner at the "Truckers Only" table. The regulars discuss current events, politics, sports, and engage in problem-solving. It's like hanging around a country barbershop. All the problems of the world are discussed and solved in less than an hour. Clarence was a fountain of knowledge, and he became the absolute arbiter of disagreements. But he went one step better when he began conducting classes. The format was simple and open. At the table he would pick up a newspaper and read the headline aloud. Then he would read and summarize the article. It wasn't always *The New York Times* or *The Chicago Tribune*. Sometimes, it was *The National Enquirer*, *The Wall Street Journal* or *The Christian Science Monitor*. He would ask if anyone wanted to comment. If there were no takers, he would give his own commentary, which was often designed to be inflammatory. In short order, he became the moderator and the regulars became the panel. He encouraged them to express their opinions, and he would offer his own based upon his studies of history, philosophy, and theology. As knowledgeable as he was, he never talked down to them.

He used the newspaper to provide the topics and the almanac to confirm the facts. He used the Bible because he liked it and wanted to apply its message to everyday events in living. He developed a following for breakfast and dinner, and the long-haul regular truckers would coordinate their schedules to enable them to participate. He gave up his felt hat for the cap with "The Professor" embroidered on it. His tweeds were left at home, and he wore plaid shirts with an assortment of team jackets. He wasn't a truck driver, but he became more like them, and they became more like him. It lasted for about ten years.

One day, he came to the clinic and told me that he needed treatment for his congestive heart failure. I asked him why he thought that, and he gave me a classical description of congestive heart failure. My examination confirmed his diagnosis, and I started him on treatment. Unfortunately, the cause of his heart failure was advanced coronary artery disease, which had severely damaged his heart. He responded well to treatment and continued conducting classes at the interstate.

One evening at his home he developed chest pain and called the paramedics. He had suffered a small heart attack, further damaging his failing heart. He recovered slowly, but he was short of breath and on the edge of heart failure. After a week, his condition was stabilized, but it was apparent that he could not return to the old house. We talked about it, and he decided to enter a nearby convalescent home until he could take care of himself in his own home.

Late one night, a week later, he called me at home. He simply stated that he wanted to be readmitted to the hospital because he knew he was going to die. He had no symptoms, but he knew he was going to die that night. As he explained this to me, he became so agitated and unreassurable that I went to the home to see him. His pulse, blood pressure, and heart rhythm were normal. He was not in heart failure. I couldn't find anything wrong with him, and I couldn't admit him to the hospital with the diagnosis, "going to die tonight!" I asked him how he knew, and he switched to his teaching mode. He explained that native American Indians had premonitions of death, often coming to them in a dream. Eskimos hear the owl call their name as a premonition of death. He went on to tell me about a tribe in Africa where tribesmen knew when they were going to die. They would simply sit under a certain tree and die. He knew he was going to die this night. I said, "If it's that sure a thing, how can anyone do anything to prevent it?" He thought about it for a short while and said, "You're right! There is nothing that you can do. It is written in 'The Book of Psalms' that the days of our life are numbered, and the years of our life are three score and ten." He was now perfectly calm and in control. He thanked me for coming and for caring for him. He said, "Good night and goodbye." The night nurse called me at six in the morning. He had been found dead in his bed.

The funeral was poorly attended by some distant relatives and a few truckers. He left his entire fortune to the Catholic Church. An auction was held and all his possessions and treasures in the old Victorian mansion were sold. The mansion itself was sold.

Over the years, the mansion deteriorated and was broken up into small apartments. There is nothing left that has the stamp and style of Clarence Cassity. I hope and believe that somewhere there is a gray-haired trucker at the dinner table reading the headlines to his grandchildren and asking them what they think.

BILLY

Outside of my family, I have had two all consuming passions. The first was being there for my patients. The second was training and competing field trial bird dogs. That is how I came to live and practice in a small country town. Unfortunately, these two passions compete for the same available time.

It was four o'clock in the morning. I was in the barn loading horses and dogs into the trailer. In two and a half hours I would be at the field trial grounds getting ready for the first brace. All I had to do was sign out to my partner and I would be gone! As I walked toward the phone, it rang! A cheery nurse from the hospital Labor and Delivery Department said, "Mrs. Calahan just came in, and she's ready to deliver." "How ready?" I asked. "Forty minutes," was the reply.

There I was: unshaven, unkempt, blue jeans, wool shirt, and "shit-kicker" boots. "Damn! It's thirty minutes to the hospital, an hour for the delivery, and thirty minutes home. I'll never make it to the grounds in time." Then it occurred to me! The hospital was on the way. I could save time. Who would know or care?

I flew down the road and parked the forty-foot rig loaded with horses and dogs in the back of the hospital parking lot. I sprinted into the service entrance and took the freight elevator up to Labor and Delivery. I scurried across the hall and made it to the doctors' dressing room, where I took off all my clothes and put on a scrub suit, mask, hat, and surgical shoes.

I scrubbed at the sink while Mrs. Calahan pushed. I walked into the delivery room just in time to catch the fourth edition of Mr. Calahan. There were no problems or complications. I checked the baby and he was fine. I wrote orders and told Mrs. Calahan I would see her the next day.

Back to the dressing room, another change of clothes and then I was on the freight elevator, which stopped on the second floor. The night supervisor and two other nurses got on. They gave no sign of greeting or recognition. In fact, they were a little concerned and kept their distance from this strange character. Apparently, they don't recognize you when you are out of uniform!

It was now five-thirty and I was on my way. "Yabba Dabba Do!"

I pulled into the parking lot at the field trial grounds at seven-thirty. It took me twenty minutes to get my horse and dog ready. At 8 a.m. I blew the whistle and turned "Meg's Boy Billy" loose in the first brace of the shooting dog event. He was a star and turned in a winning performance.

That evening, driving home with the trophy and the dog in my lap, I marveled about what a wonderful day it had been. I truly had it all. I had my cake and was eating it too.

The next morning I made early rounds at the hospital. I gave a smiling "good morning" to the three nurses of the freight elevator, and they responded in kind, with no reference to our previous meeting. Mrs. Calahan was fine and asked how I did at the trials. I told her in delicious detail how we had won.

We talked a while, and she asked if I had any suggestions for the boy's name as she had used up all the good ones. I instantly replied, "Billy." William Shane Calahan is now about thirty years old. I don't know if he knows who he is named after.

ANIMAL HUSBANDRY

The two of them sat in the office, both quiet, one tense. The father wore bib overalls and "shit-kicker" boots. He had a two-day beard stubble. He was a livestock farmer. The son was similarly attired and stared blankly at the floor. He was not quite right. He appeared to be about eighteen and had a quarter-inch crew cut for cleanliness. He was big; taller than six feet and weighed about two hundred ninety pounds. His mouth was half open revealing his large tongue, which protruded through it. His teeth were stained and decayed.

My first question is always the same, "How can I help you?" The father looked me square in the eye and said, "I want him gelded." In all my years of practicing family medicine, that was the only time I received that reply. The father was in earnest. I asked why he wanted to have the boy castrated, but in my heart I already knew. The son never looked up as the father continued. "As a boy, he was no trouble and he was easy to manage. But when his hormones came in, he became uncontrollable. He got big and mean and stronger than me. At first he used to 'jerk off' a lot, and I figured that was good because it would help to

50

take the pressure off. We live out aways, and we don't see many people, and keeping him on the farm was safe enough. But my little girl is now fifteen, and her hormones are in. He's so damn strong I had to use a baseball bat to get him off her last week. I can't be there all the time, and sooner or later he's going to get her or someone else. Then I guess I'd have to shoot him." This man had simple answers for complicated problems.

I had lived in a city almost all my life and knew nothing of animal husbandry. The natural question was, "Would castration really help?" There was no doubt in his mind. "We castrate stallions, and they become tractable, easy to handle, and ignore the mares. We take young bulls and cut 'em, and the steers pay no attention to the heifers. They're not irritable and are easy to deal with." I told him that I was sure that it was against the law to do what he suggested, but that I would inquire and find out if we could get a court order to do it. He laughed and said that we would just be spinning our wheels, and that nothing would come of it. "The courts never try to solve problems until the shit hits the fan, and then it's too late. You can bet I'll hear from the courts after I kill him." He was deadly serious, and I didn't know what to do. I told him that I would look into the matter and get back to him. He took the boy and left. It was only after they had left that I realized I had never spoken to the young man and didn't know if he could speak or understand.

I tossed and turned all night as the problem kept reappearing in my mind. I had no doubt that the father would kill him and probably go to jail. If the story was true, the daughter as well as her girlfriends were in great danger. Someone had to do something to avoid this impending catastrophe.

I went to the library and found that several states allowed castration to be performed on violent sexual offenders. But that was always done after the fact.

I called a civil judge I knew and presented a "hypothetical case." He said, "No way in hell would the courts order or allow a castration to be done on a retarded boy. Furthermore, the boy is only guilty of being retarded." He suggested that I have a psychiatric social worker get involved and consider putting him in a state residential institution. Institutionalizing him didn't seem like a good idea either.

I called the father and talked about placing the boy in a state institution, but he would not consider it. "The boy is happy here on the farm. The problem is the sex drive thing." I asked the father to bring the boy in again for me to talk with and examine.

I asked the farmer to leave the room so that I could talk to the boy alone. His appearance was the same. He stared blankly at the floor and avoided eye contact with me. He did not answer when I asked his name and what he did, but he followed instructions when I asked him to undress and get up on the exam table. I talked and invited answers to questions, but he never said a word. He did not appear to be frightened. I started my exam. When I touched him, he grabbed my hands in his and almost broke them. I asked him to let go, with more than a touch of panic in my voice. He looked me squarely in the eye, smiled and slowly released my hands. I completed the exam without further incident and found no specific pathology. His lab tests were normal including his thyroid, testosterone, and steroid levels. I was no closer to solving the problem than before.

I went to see my mentor, an older more experienced family doctor, for whom I had enormous respect. I presented the case to him, and after a little thought he replied, "Fix his hernias." I didn't know what he was talking about. Besides, the boy didn't have hernias. He went on and said, "When doing a hernia repair, one must be very careful not to damage the testicular artery. If it is ligated, the testicle will atrophy and slowly disappear, and testosterone levels will fall dramatically."

I had the answer, but did I have the courage? The risks to me and my career were enormous. For one thing, without the patient's permission or a court order, this was essentially a criminal act. Its morality could be argued both ways. To deceive my hospital and circumvent its rules and regulations were unconscionable, and if found out, I would lose my hospital privileges. Was this a medical problem or a societal problem?

I just couldn't do it.

I met with the boy's father again and referred him to a psychiatric social worker. He was furious with me and stomped out of the office. For more than a year afterward I scanned the local paper looking for his name and a story involving rape and murder, but none appeared. In fact, I never heard of him again.

CAN WE TALK?

Teenage sexuality has always been of great concern to me. I personally would prefer that they not be sexually active. However, I am a realist and recognize the power of biological drives. Teenage pregnancy is a catastrophe and, consequently, I have always offered contraceptive advice to all teenagers with or without their parent's knowledge or approval.

In the early part of my career, pregnant teenagers either married, which I discouraged, or put their babies up for adoption, which I encouraged. In recent years, pregnant teenagers married less frequently and either had abortions, or they had and kept their babies. Those who married usually compounded their problems, and the effects on the women and their babies were disastrous. Those who remained single and kept their babies had a decidedly limited future. Those who elected abortion had to deal with the emotional crisis. As can be seen, the pregnant teenager has only four options, three of which are poor, and one which is used infrequently. We must be more aggressive in preventing teen pregnancy.

In Illinois, state law mandates that all students entering high school are to have an examination by a physician. Most of these students are approximately fourteen years old, which is a year earlier than the age at which most students reportedly become sexually active. The school physical is a perfect time for the physician to intervene and educate these vulnerable young men and women.

There is a marvelous pamphlet entitled, "NO and Other Methods of Birth Control." It compares all of the known methods of birth control, including saying "No," as to effectiveness, side effects, risks, and benefits. It is a treasure trove of sexual information for teenagers who are either misinformed or uninformed. Unfortunately, it does not talk enough about sexually transmitted diseases, which is yet another problem.

In my practice, I would introduce the subject of sexuality at the time of the high school exam. I would give the students, male or female, the pamphlet to take home and to read, preferably with one of their parents. I would also clearly state to the young women that if they were sexually active or thought they would be, I would prescribe birth control for them without involving their parents.

Over the years, I received a few telephone calls from irate parents, but they were very infrequent. I believe that this aggressive approach is effective in preventing teen pregnancy. Of course there are always failures for a variety of reasons, but not because of ignorance.

It has been said that sex is like the weather. Everybody talks about it, but nobody does anything about it. I believe the opposite is true. Everybody is "doing" sex, but nobody talks about it. We cannot ignore reality and must protect these young people.

ODDS

Odd accidents happen all the time and seem to be orchestrated by a malevolent force. It's no wonder that people believe in evil spirits and bad luck. What are the odds of any of the following incidents ever happening again?

The broken shaft of a golf club protruded out both sides of his leg and the blood oozed down to puddle on the floor. I put a tourniquet on his leg and arranged to transfer him to a vascular surgeon at the hospital. "How did this happen?" I asked. He replied, "I missed a seven iron and lost my cool. I got so mad that I threw the club. It hit a passing golf cart which broke off the head and threw the shaft back like a spear. I don't know if I'm lucky or not."

A teenager had been striking the heads of two hammers together because he liked to hear the sound. It was a hot summer day, and he was wearing a bathing suit. All of a sudden, he had terrible pain in his penis, and when he looked down, bright red blood was soaking through his suit. I examined him at the clinic. I found a perforation in the head of the penis and could feel a piece of metal

57

embedded below the surface. After putting in a local block, I removed a metal shard that looked just like a small arrowhead and fit exactly into a defect in one of the hammerheads.

It was breakfast time and she was in her bare feet preparing food when a knife fell off the counter, blade down, embedding itself in the top of her foot. The blade slipped into an eighth of an inch space between two bones and severed the main artery in the top of the foot. It was as if a maliciously mad surgeon, deliberately and with great skill, cut the artery. The incision was only a quarter of an inch long.

Before coming to Our Town, I was a flight surgeon in the United States Air Force, stationed in the Far East. An aircraft had been lost at sea, and a single body was recovered from a life raft floating in the Sea of Japan. We did the necessary examinations and studies and prepared the body for return to the States on a military cargo plane. That aircraft was also lost at sea and nothing was recovered.

He was sitting in his office, behind a desk, in a brick building at the bottom of a long steep hill. A runaway dump truck, which had lost its brakes, crashed through the wall and buried him in sand.

No place is safe!

TIMING

The Lewis and Clark Expedition (1804–1806) lost only one man, who died of appendicitis near St. Louis. Calvin Coolidge, thirtieth President of the United States, lost his only son to blood poisoning, which started as a blister on his heel after playing tennis. Frank Klusky died in Our Town in 1963 of coronary artery disease. All of these people would have survived had their illnesses occurred now.

Timing is everything in life.

I practiced during the "golden age" of medicine. Scientific and technical progress has exploded in the past forty years to such a degree that it can be said that ninety percent of what physicians know and do today, was not known and could not have been done forty years ago. It is not only that people are surviving and living longer, but are doing so in comfort. Talk to someone with a hip replacement. We accept joint replacements and organ transplants as commonplace today. These things were considered miraculous when they were first done.

I recently saw a list of the major medical achievements of the past thirty years, all of which are done every day in hospitals throughout the country. Alongside that list, I created another list of people's names, people in my practice who would have lived, and lived well, if that technology had been available to them. It was a considerable list. No wonder we have such a large aged population. Life expectancy went from sixty-eight years in 1950 to seventy-six years in 1990 and it is still rising!

I have always had the fantasy of living in this country at the beginning of the western expansion. I have dreamed of being with Lewis and Clark. I have yearned to be with the early mountain men. But in all probability, I would have died of cholera or typhoid at an early age and would have been buried in an unmarked grave.

So much for timing.

ENBRUJADA

José Garcia was a good-looking "macho man." He was married and had two children. He worked at the local mill as a laborer.

It was his custom to visit his parents in Mexico for two weeks each year. Usually the whole family went, but this year he went by himself because they didn't want to take the children out of school. Besides, his wife wasn't too fond of his parents, and they didn't care much for her either!

He returned from Mexico two weeks ago and now sat in my office avoiding eye contact. He spoke quietly and mumbled. I had to ask him several times to speak up and repeat what he had said. I asked, "How was the trip?" His reply, "I got trouble." I suspected a familiar scenario. The husband goes away on a trip, gets sexually involved with a stranger, and comes home overwhelmed by guilt and the fear of venereal disease. He usually has some vague symptoms but rarely a venereal disease. His main problem is guilt, and he feels he has to talk with somebody about it. I got right to the point asking, "What kind of trouble?" He said, "Enbrujada, The Evil Eye."

The story unfolded that he had spent a few days with his parents and then moved in with an old girlfriend in the town where he had grown up. He looked upon it as part of the entertainment for his vacation. Unfortunately, the young woman took it as a commitment. When he told her he was returning to the States, she became furious, cursed him, and cast a spell on him with "The Evil Eye." When he returned to his wife, he was impotent.

In my mind his impotence was the result of his fear and guilt, and I was confident that it would correct itself. He simply needed to talk about it and be forgiven. We talked about the matter for sometime, but he denied any feelings of guilt. I forgave him anyway.

However, his impotence did not improve. He confessed to his wife and obtained her forgiveness. But he remained impotent.

I performed a complete medical workup and could not demonstrate any cause for his impotence. I gave a trial of testosterone, and he tried unsuccessfully to have intercourse with other women, but still remained limp. In desperation, I referred him to a urologist but he had no suggestions.

Finally, José announced that he was going back to Mexico where the spell had been put on him. He would see a local witch doctor for treatment. I wished him well as there certainly was nothing I could do for him.

He was back in a week, grinning from ear to ear. One session with the witch doctor had solved the problem. Needless to say, he didn't visit his old girlfriend.

To my knowledge, he has remained faithful to his wife ever since. Who would believe that an eye could have such power?

LIFE'S NOT FAIR

President Jimmy Carter made the observation that life is not always fair. Physicians have always known that life is a lottery.

She was sixteen and sitting in my office. She sparkled. It was not only that she was physically beautiful, but she was intelligent, athletic, and charming. She was not ill, but was in the office for a sports physical exam required by her high school. She was a serious tennis player as well as a winning golfer. With all this going for her, she was also a successful student. I am sure she made the young men nervous and the women envious.

She came to the office infrequently, but I was always impressed by her presence. I wanted to introduce her to one of my sons, but she was not interested. I would occasionally read in the local papers about some of her successes: winning a scholarship, winning a tournament. Then there was her engagement announcement, accompanied by a photograph. It seemed so all-American. They looked just like Ken and Barbie. They married and moved to a nearby town where they both had good jobs. I lost track of her and didn't see or hear anything about her for several years.

It was early in the morning, and I was making rounds when the emergency room paged me. They had a patient for me to examine. She was unconscious on the table. Her face was swollen and unrecognizable with bloody lacerations and abrasions. An endotracheal tube had been placed, an IV was running, and she was stable.

She had been driving to work that morning and had been broadsided by a loaded dump truck. Her door had popped open and she was thrown out, landing on her face. She bounced across the asphalt until her head struck the curb, stopping her forward motion. The event lasted only seconds and it was done.

It took several hours for the team to clean her face and remove the gravel and road debris. Tissue that was nonviable was removed and the lacerations closed. Her face was grossly swollen, round as a pumpkin, and oozing bloody fluid. It was blue in places and blood-red in others. It appeared as if she had been sandblasted. But this was the least of her problems.

She was comatose and her breathing was assisted by a ventilator. Her head injury was severe, and her brain was damaged.

The intensive care team supported her, maintained her fluids, controlled her seizures, transfused her, protected her skin, and sucked the secretions from her airway. She was fed through a gastrostomy tube. Eventually her breathing stabilized and the ventilator and endotracheal tube were removed. But she did not wake up! Days and weeks went by. The family hovered expectantly, but nothing happened.

On the twenty-eighth day she opened her eyes and looked blankly around the room, recognizing no one. Within days her arms and legs, which had been maintained with physical therapy, began to move spontaneously. She spent more time awake and was able to swallow. The stomach tube was removed. Speech came very slowly; it was guttural and in a monotone. She was transferred to a large rehabilitation center, and over a six-month period, she made excellent progress. She was able to walk and had reasonable hand control, but she would never play golf or tennis again. Her speech improved, but it was slow as it took time for her to find the words. She had lost her sense of humor and was dull. No one would ever call her charming or vivacious again. However, she was functioning and her rehab therapists were pleased. But all who knew her from before the accident grieved because the light of her spirit had gone out and would not come back.

Her marriage lasted another two years. Her husband really tried, but this was not the woman he had married. She moved to another state to live with her parents. I never heard of her again.

When I think of her, I always go back to when she was sixteen and sparkled.

OLD COUNTRY

The Bozych brothers lived in a different world. They came to America during the Polish migration and bought a farm near Our Town. They had been farmers in a small isolated community in "the old country" and were quite self-sufficient. Almost everything they used, they produced or grew themselves.

The farmhouse was made of quarry stone. They built it themselves. It was primitive, lacking indoor plumbing and, for a while, electricity. They were grain farmers, but they kept cows, steers, and pigs, mainly for their own use with some for the local market. The chicken coop supplied them with eggs and poultry. The orchard and the garden gave fruit and vegetables until the first hard frost. They even had a pond and their own icehouse. There was a still in the barn, and they made their own corn whiskey. They hardly ever came to town and no one visited them.

They were the stereotype of the old-time bachelor farmers. They lived in bib overalls, which were hardly ever washed. When they got too rotten to wear, they replaced them with new ones ordered from the Sears catalogue. Long johns were put on in the fall and not changed until spring. They actually believed that washing their whole body was unhealthy. (Maybe that's true. They both lived well into their eighties.) Needless to say, they looked bad and smelled bad. They couldn't care less. When I would chastise them about how they lived, they would laugh and quip, "Hey, we got it good here. You should have seen us in the old country."

Their lives were limited and divided into three parts. They worked the farm every day. They drank corn whiskey when the work was done and eventually tumbled into bed for sleep. The farm was productive, and they made a lot of money with which they bought additional land to farm. They spent no money on themselves. They eventually built up a huge estate for God knows who.

I met them in August of 1963. I had a new bird dog, and I was working him through the fields in a training session on a Sunday morning. It was getting quite warm when the dog went over a hill and disappeared. I was very concerned lest he get heat stroke, and I quickened my pace. I topped the hill and saw their farm for the first time.

The place was a mess. The house was a square stone building with a rusting galvanized roof. Old vehicles and rusting farm equipment lay about in disarray. There were outbuildings everywhere. Chickens and ducks wandered about as they pleased. Cattle, horses, and pigs seemed to live in a commune. The smell of manure floated up the hill.

There was a large shade tree in front of the house. Under the tree, two old men sat on kitchen chairs swigging whiskey from a jug kept cool in a tub of ice water. My dog was in the tub, getting his ears rubbed as he drank the cold water. They waved me in and offered me the jug.

We sat, talked, and drank. They wanted to know who I was and what I did. I explained that I was a new doctor in town. They picked up my accent (New York City) and asked, "How long you been this country?" I told them I had come to Our Town last June. They were impressed and said, "Hey, you speak pretty good English for a greenhorn." We became friends. They and the farm became regular stops on dog training days.

Until their final illness, neither brother was hardly ever sick. I went to the farm when the older brother had pneumonia. After I examined him and prescribed treatment, he asked, "How much do I owe you?" I told him, "Ten dollars." He removed a large stone from the wall and took out a cash box that was crammed with greenbacks. He rummaged through the box and gave me a ten dollar bill. It was an old ten dollar gold certificate. I had never seen one before, but they assured me that it was real money.

Years later, when they were gone and the farm abandoned, I sat under the shade tree with another dog and thought about them. I went into the falling-down house and pulled out the stone. There was nothing there, just a hole in the wall.

DING-A-LINGS

The telephone is indispensable to the efficient practice of medicine. It can instantly connect the patient to his physician. I have always felt that instant access was important and that a successful family practice depended on it. Consequently, for all of my career, I or one of my partners, was accessible by telephone at all times. There was no end to the telephone calls. There were hundreds of thousands of them. Most of them were straightforward and appropriate, but some were different.

2:00 A.M.: Ding-a-ling — Ding-a-ling

"Hello, my name is Mrs. Peterson and I am a patient of Doctor Carter." (A physician with whom I had no coverage relationship. In fact, he was a competitor.) For a week now I have been waking up at two in the morning with this terrible burning in my chest. I'm belching and nauseated, and I'm afraid I'm going to vomit. What should I do?" I replied, "Mrs. Peterson, if Doctor Carter is your doctor, why don't you call him?" She replied, "I would,

70

except the poor man works so hard, I hate to wake him up." I did not lose my cool. I remained calm and explained, "I know Doctor Carter. He really worries about his patients, and he would be very upset to know that you called me. I suggest you call him right now." She thanked me and hung up. By now I was wide awake, somewhat agitated, and had plenty of heartburn of my own. I couldn't sleep, so I made 6 a.m. rounds at the hospital where I ran into Doctor Carter and told him the story. He laughed and said he wished all his patients felt that way.

11:00 P.M.: Ding-a-ling — Ding-a-ling

"Hello Doctor, this is an emergency! My mother fell down the stairs and is unconscious on the floor. Can you come right now?" Without a thought I replied, "Give me the address and I'll be right out." The address he gave was on an out-of-the-way side street. He did not give me his name, and I did not recognize his voice. I felt very uneasy, and before I left home I called the police and asked them to meet me at the address. We arrived at the same time with the squad car's dome lights flashing. As we pulled up, four people ran out of the back of the house and disappeared in the darkness. The house was abandoned and empty. I had been set up as a mark.

In the years that followed, I continued to make house calls to families that I knew, but I always had the police meet me at the houses of strangers.

3:00 A.M.: Ding-a-ling — Ding-a-ling

"Doctor, is it all right to give a four-month-old baby regular milk?" I replied, "At three in the morning it certainly is."

4:00 A.M.: Ding-a-ling — Ding-a-ling

"Doctor, I'm glad I caught you before you left the house. I want to make an appointment for nine o'clock this morning."

10:00 P.M.: Ding-a-ling — Ding-a-ling

"Doctor Ladd, I know you are having an affair with my wife. I know where you live and how you come and go. I'm going to get you."

9:00 P.M.: Ding-a-ling — Ding-a-ling

"Doctor, you don't know me, but I am a patient of Doctor Jones, and I have bone cancer. I'm in a lot of pain and my Talwin has run out. Doctor Jones is out of town. Could you please call the pharmacy and order up some more." I told him, "I'm sorry, I can't order narcotics for a patient I have never seen. Call the doctor that covers Doctor Jones when he is gone. He will have your records and will help you." The caller replied, "I did call him, but he doesn't return my calls, and the pain is terrible. I need something now." "I can't help you," I said. "Why don't you have someone take you to the emergency room of the hospital where you were a patient. They will have records on you and will be able to help you with your pain." The reply was, "I'm alone and have no way to get to the hospital. I told him, "I'm sorry, I can't give you narcotics, but I will get you something else for your pain and have the pharmacy deliver it to you." "No!" he said. "I have to have Talwin." "Well, I'm sorry, but I can't help you." "Thank you, doctor."

9:00 P.M.: Ding-a-ling — Ding-a-ling

"Doctor, I need you to help me with my crabby wife." I replied that my own wife was pretty crabby and that there wasn't much I could do about it. "You don't understand," he said, "she really is crabby." I said, "Crabby is crabby. I didn't know there were degrees of crabbiness." "Listen," he said, "My wife has the crabs, and we both need treatment." I said, "Ohhh!"

1:00 A.M.: Ding-a-ling — Ding-a-ling

"You remember me? I'm the guy that applied for social security disability and you refused to say I was disabled. You better watch your back. I'm going to break your legs with a baseball bat and then you can apply for social security disability."

VICKS

I love to watch mothers and their young children. If their relationship is positive, they are constantly communicating with each other on a nonverbal level. The message is trust and love. I think neither of them is aware of this.

The mother will be talking to me and unconsciously stroking her daughter's hair. The two-year-old standing next to his mother will be looking at me with suspicion, holding on to his mother's leg or peering from behind her body. As the two of them sit together, they kind of lean into each other, and there is much touching and stroking. I sometimes tease the mother with, "I caught you loving your baby." It's all so spontaneous and beautiful.

I love my children. My mother loved me, and her mother loved her, just as you, hopefully, have loved and have been loved. Mothers would often bring in a sick child, and in the history would volunteer that she had "rubbed him up good with Vicks." I always asked if her mother had also rubbed her with Vicks, and it was always so.

Vicks rub-on products have a characteristic pleasant medicinal smell. That smell reminds tens of millions of people that their mothers loved them. Vicks has been around for more than a hundred years. That means that four generations of children have been "rubbed up good with Vicks." That aroma stands as a testament to their mothers' love, and they in turn perpetuate that love by applying it to their children.

I do not know what therapeutic pharmaceuticals are in Vicks products. I do know it would be a terrible thing if they omitted the aroma, and I'm sure it would be less effective and less marketable.

GOD'S WILL

Penny was a "biker" girl. She had a yellow "Titty Bear" tattooed on her right breast and a small red rose just above the bikini line in her groin. Her long hair, in a single braid, and dangling earrings gave her an exotic appearance. She was warm and friendly with a white toothy smile.

She was recently married and came to the office for a general exam. She had been on birth control pills for several years and wanted to get off them now, "to give her body a rest." This was a common misconception, and I explained to her that as long as she was having no problems with her pills, there was no reason to stop them. I also explained that while she was "resting her body," she might wake up pregnant. Her reply was that her mother had used a diaphragm for many years and had three planned pregnancies. Therefore, she wanted to be fitted for a diaphragm. I pointed out that diaphragms had a ten percent failure rate, and that it was even higher in young women with no children. "So be it," she said. "If I get pregnant, it's God's will."

It is time consuming and a little messy to fit a diaphragm and to teach women how to use it correctly. The measuring rings come in a kit with eight diaphragms, each one five millimeters larger in diameter than the one in front of it. The physician starts by inserting the average size diaphragm into the vagina and working the sizes up or down until the best fit is obtained. These fitting rings are exactly like the diaphragm the patient will use, except that each one has a half-inch hole punched in the center. I fitted her properly and twice she demonstrated that she could insert it correctly. I gave her a prescription for a 70mm Ortho-Allflex Diaphragm Kit with a book of instructions and wished her well.

About thirty minutes after the patient left, my nurse asked what I had done with the 70mm measuring ring. It was missing. I said, "I left it in the sink." "Well, it's not there," she replied. "I think Penny took it home." I didn't comment and Barbara pressed me with, "Don't you think we ought to call and tell her?" "It's God's will," I replied.

Six months later Penny was back in my office having missed two periods. She was indeed pregnant. I asked her if she had been using the diaphragm I had prescribed. She said, "No. It's just too much trouble to mess with. Besides, it's time I settled down and had a family."

TARANTELLA

The Tarantella is a lively Italian dance and Giuseppe (Joe) Tarantella was certainly a lively little Italian. He emigrated to this country as a child after World War Two and grew up in Our Town. He finished high school and worked at the steel mill. He was a hard worker and everybody liked Joe. He charmed the pants off of Josephine, and they were married in the "German Catholic Church."

Our Town was different from other places. We had a church on every hill and a tavern on every corner. The churches and the taverns were basically the social centers of the community. Considerable time and money were spent by the same people in both places.

It was the custom of working men to stop at the tavern on the way home from work to "drink a few with the boys." Some would stop there before work. In the evening, men and their wives or girlfriends would dance and sing and socialize at the tavern.

Joe was the life of the party. He could drink with the best of them. He could get wild and sing and dance all night. He was funny and made people laugh, and people enjoyed being with him. At the mill he was a laborer. At the tavern he was a star.

Josie, on the other hand, was quiet. She didn't like the limelight. She would rather have stayed at home. There was too much commotion at the tavern. Really too much of everything: too much noise, too much drinking, too many fights. Her pregnancy gave her the excuse to stay home. I suppose that was the beginning of the end. She stayed home every night while he partied at the tavern. She told herself that it would be all right. He was a man and he should be out with his friends. After all, he truly loved her.

This scenario continued for six years and four children. Josie's life was "*Kinder, Kirche,* and *Kuchen.*" That, to Josie, was good because that is how it had been for her mother, and she had been brought up that way. However, she would have liked it better if Joe spent more time with her and the kids. But he was there on Sundays. He was a good provider, and she was content.

Joe, on the other hand, was not content. He thought his wife was dull, unattractive, and stupid. She was nothing compared to the young women that frequented the tavern, and in time, he charmed the pants off of them too.

He was unhappy in his job. There was no future there. He drank too much and became argumentative. One night he got his nose broken and another time he was cut. Josie told him he should stay out of the tavern and stay home with her, so he blackened both of her eyes. He stayed irritable. She could not reason with him about anything. Every time she disagreed with him, he beat her up. Soon, she was glad he spent most of his time in the tavern and little time at home. However, he spent enough time at home to give her a dose of the "clap."

I treated her gonorrhea in the office, and he came in later for shots. I asked her why she stayed married to him when he beats her, cheats on her, and gives her venereal disease. Her answer was straightforward. "I have four children, no skills, and he brings home a paycheck. I can't make it without him." I suggested marriage counseling, and she looked at me as if I were crazy. I told her that unless she did something about the situation, the beatings would get worse.

One day Joe got into an argument with his foreman at work, which degenerated into a brawl, and he was fired. He tried, unsuccessfully, to get another job and after about three months just gave up trying.

Josie's mother made sure they didn't go hungry and kept a roof over their heads. She wouldn't give them any money because she knew Joe would take it to the tavern. Josie got a job at the bottling plant on the assembly line. It was the first, full-time paid job she ever had. She loved it. She not only enjoyed the work, she thrived on the camaraderie with the other women. She knew she had to give Joe some of the money, just enough to keep him content at the tavern and away from her.

The job was good and Josie was good at it. When given the opportunity, she demonstrated leadership and organizational skills. Over time she became a supervisor and part of management. She never told Joe how well she was doing nor how much money she was making. She continued to give him his allowance.

She returned home from grocery shopping on a Saturday morning. He was waiting for her in the kitchen. He had the stub of her salary check in his hand and was enraged. "You make all this money and give me pennies." He hit her alongside the head with a closed fist. "All this money," he shouted and hit her again and again. She went down on the floor. Her nose was bleeding, and she had a cut over her left eye. He kept shouting, "all this money," and kicked her over and over again until she didn't move anymore. He threw the check stub onto the bloody floor and stormed out. An eight-year-old child called the police for help.

She barely survived. Her spleen was ruptured and had to be removed. She had facial fractures that had to be elevated and several fractured ribs. She required six units of blood.

She did not press charges. Joe came to the hospital and cried and pleaded for forgiveness. "It was the drink. I love you." She told him that it was over and that she was finished with him. She and the kids were going to move in with her mother, and if he came around, she would kill him. A nurse, who witnessed their conversation, told me that Josie said it so calmly and quietly that she had no doubt that Josie would do it.

On the way home from the hospital, Josie and her mother stopped at the gun shop and picked up a twenty-five caliber Beretta pistol with as much emotion as picking up two quarts of milk and a loaf of bread.

They brought Joe to our emergency room. He was agitated and shouting, "I can't believe she did this to me, the father of her children." She had fired at him twice, and although she missed what she was aiming for, both bullets hit him. One embedded itself in his groin and the other passed clear through his inner thigh.

Joe never bothered her again and had nothing to do with the family. He did odd jobs around town to get enough money to drink. He ate and slept wherever he could. He continued to drink heavily and died in his early forties of cirrhosis.

WALLPAPER

Like everyone else, I too have sat in a doctor's examining room, staring at the walls, waiting for him to appear. Unless you bring your own reading material, the only other source of diversion is to read the certificates on the wall.

It's reassuring to know he graduated from medical school and has a license to practice medicine. It makes me feel more comfortable to read that he is "board certified" in his specialty. But what about the other twenty certificates?

I see he took a course in the Bahamas on communication skills. There is a certificate that tells me he attended a seminar in Maui on family counseling. There is a certificate for sports medicine, another for proctoscopy, and still another for having expertise in cryosurgery!

Is all this necessary? Is he covering holes in the wall? It should be sufficient that he graduated medical school, has a license, and is board certified.

In my practice, I displayed my M.D. degree, my license, and my board certification. I did, however, add my "Circle Pines Nursery" diploma. I did that because I loved

Mrs. Brennan, my kindergarten teacher. I hung it alongside my M.D. degree. The certificates were dated exactly twenty years apart (1938 – 1958).

That left my walls quite bare and boring. The patients had very little to read.

The printed word has great power, the power to teach and inspire. My brother-in-law does calligraphy. He and I conspired to cover the walls with beautiful messages.

Often, I would come into the room and see patients writing them down in order to remember them and to share them with others. I never saw anyone copying my license, my degree, nor my nursery school diploma.

These are a few samples:

> *"There is a destiny that makes us brothers.*
> *None goes his way alone.*
> *All that we send into the lives of others,*
> *Comes back into our own."*

> *"Today is the first day of the rest of my life.*
> *I shall begin anew."*

> *"I am one of two billion people on this planet*
> *of which there are eight [sic]*
> *Rotating around the sun in a small galaxy*
> *of which there are an infinite number.*
> *Therefore it makes no difference if I have beans or peas*
> *for supper."*

My favorite is:

*"The most important thing a father can do for his children
is to love their mother."*

COMPASSION

Recently, the news media has been full of Doctor Jack Kevorkian. He is a retired pathologist in Michigan who has been assisting suffering, terminally ill patients to commit suicide. It is an act of human compassion and requires great courage on the part of the doctor. He not only exposes himself to criminal prosecution, but to the vehemence and possible violence of those who strongly oppose his views and consider him an unrestrained murderer.

The Hemlock Society advocates the option of suicide for suffering terminally ill patients. In the past few years there have been self-help books on the market instructing people in how to end their own lives. These books are tragic and inappropriate. Many of the people who use them to commit suicide do not have terminal illnesses. They can be treated and helped.

That we are hearing so much about assisted suicide now, demonstrates that it is indeed a problem that needs to be addressed. The reality that medical technology can keep people alive without necessarily improving the quality of

86

their lives, means that the problem of dealing with the suffering, terminally ill will get worse.

I do not have the answer for the nation. Eventually the medical ethicists and the government will establish legal guidelines for assisted suicide that we can all live or die with. I do have the answer for myself and my patients.

My mission has always been to relieve suffering and to restore the patient to his previous level of health, comfort, and function. That is not always possible. Many illnesses are incurable and progressive. The patient cannot maintain his health, comfort, or function. But he should not have to suffer on the road to death!

When people think of the suffering, terminally ill patient, they are usually thinking of someone with advanced incurable cancer. We cannot cure him, but we can certainly help him. We can and should relieve him of his pain.

Early in the course of the disease, pain pills usually suffice. As the disease becomes more widespread and painful, the oral dose is increased to control the pain. Different physical modalities such as permanent nerve block can be used. Different narcotics can be given orally, rectally, or by needle. The patient and family members need to learn how to give narcotics by injection as the patient needs it. There is certainly no concern that the patient will become an addict. The patient is dying.

Eventually, the amount of narcotic required to relieve the pain gets close to a lethal dose, and the patient may overdose and die. So be it.

SLEEP

Sleep deprivation is the normal state for family doctors in small towns. They are well-conditioned and adapted to that state. During their internships and residencies, they often had long work schedules, including being on-call and available for thirty-six hours and off for twelve. They slept when and where they could. However, there are limits to just how much you can do without sleep.

I had been working almost nonstop for two days, and I was exhausted. Unfortunately, I was still on-call. When I answer the phone from a sound sleep, it takes me a while to be alert enough to comprehend what the patient is saying. On the other hand, the patient is wide awake and alert when making the call.

The phone rang and I answered it. The caller immediately presented the problem. I don't know exactly what transpired. All I can remember is saying, "And give him a nice warm glass of milk," as I hung up the phone. Then I was instantly awake. I had no idea to whom I had talked or what the problem had been. I prayed for the person to call back. I hoped that it had been an insignificant problem and not an impending medical catastrophe. As tired as I was, it was a sleepless night.

The next day, a woman brought in her febrile child. She asked me if I was all right. She told me that she had called at one o'clock in the morning about her child's 104-degree fever, and that I had given her some nonsensical advice and hung up. She went on to suggest that I looked bad, and that I should get more sleep.

One of my colleagues was always accessible to his patients, and for most of his career he practiced by himself. Consequently, he or his wife were on call all the time. The telephone was on her side of the bed. She would answer it and give medical advice freely, allowing the doctor to sleep and, hopefully, keep him from going out into the night.

The phone rang at 2 a.m., and Mrs. Bryant answered it. A woman on the other end of the line said that her child had the croup. Mrs. Bryant covered the phone and whispered to her groggy husband, "Croup." He whispered back, and Mrs. Bryant instructed the mother to put the child in the bathroom and run the hot shower on the cold wall to create mist. That should help. The woman replied that she had done that and the child's breathing was better, but the cough was severe. Mrs. Bryant covered the phone and whispered, "severe cough." He whispered back, "cough syrup," which Mrs. Bryant relayed to the mother. The mother replied by saying she had done that, but the cough persisted, and now the child had a 102-degree fever. Mrs. Bryant started to cover the phone to relay the information when the mother spoke up, "Mrs. Bryant! If that man in bed with you is a doctor, can I talk to him." Mrs. Bryant never said a word and handed over the phone.

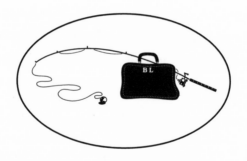

SLEEPING BEAUTY

The passage from childhood to adulthood is a dangerous and difficult journey. Teenagers by their very nature
may self-destruct as they go from total dependence to inde-
pendence. They are hard to deal with and almost impossible to live with. They are driven by hormones, peer
pressure, and the ever-present media. Yet, all of the things
we find most disagreeable in teenagers, their impulsiveness,
irresponsibility, rebelliousness, and secretiveness are really
normal behavior. It is amazing that so many of us adults
have survived that journey unharmed. Young adults in
their twenties, thinking back on their teenage years, can
hardly believe how they behaved, nor can they explain
why they were that way.

One of the major problems of teenagers is their inability to see the possible consequences of their actions. They
feel indestructible and seem to believe that bad things
happen only to other people. They are dead wrong. They
die in automobile wrecks because of alcohol and excessive
speed. They die of drug overdoses. They get into situations

where they decide the only solution is suicide. Your town is no different than Our Town.

Rose Ann was seventeen. She was a delightful teenager: the all-American girl, the girl next door, like your kid sister or your niece, or perhaps your daughter or your granddaughter.

The party was at a friend's house; the parents were out of town. The event was forbidden, but who would know? Who would tell? The word spread through the high school, "Party at Judy's house." What started out as a small get-together, involved almost a hundred teenagers, all good kids like yours and mine. They had music and dancing. They had pot and booze. It was a bring-your-own-bottle party. Some brought pop, others brought beer, and still others brought gin and vodka.

Rose Ann was excited. What a party! The music was terrific, and Glenn was such a hunk. They danced and she took a few hits from a joint. It relaxed her and she could dance better. She drank some vodka and orange juice, and it made her feel good. Normally, she was a little shy and introverted, but not tonight. She and Glenn were dancing up a storm. She began drinking the vodka straight out of the bottle. It went down so easy and she felt so good. She was talking funny now, and everyone laughed. She was the hit of the party, but now she was so tired. The room was turning, and she didn't feel good anymore. Glenn took her out on the front lawn to get some fresh air, but it didn't help. She lay down on the ground and went to sleep. Glenn tried to wake her up, but she just lay there.

"What to do? What to do?"

They loaded her into a car. Glenn was driving.

"Where to go? Where to go?"

"We can't take her to the hospital; they will ask too many questions. We can't take her home; her father will kill us."

They drove her home, but not quite. They left her unconscious body on the grass in the front of her house as if by magic she would get up and go inside. Fred Wallace was walking his dog and saw her body on the lawn. He tried to wake her up, and when he couldn't, he rang the doorbell. They called the paramedics.

I saw her in the emergency room. She was in a deep coma. She had no reflexes and no muscle tone. She was barely breathing, and then she stopped breathing altogether. She was "Sleeping Beauty" without a "Prince Charming" who would wake her with a kiss. We intubated her and connected her to a ventilator that breathed for her, but nothing else changed. Her blood alcohol level was 1300 mg% (800 mg% is enough to cause death; 100 mg% is considered drunk). It takes a long time for the body to process alcohol, to detoxify it, and remove it from the system. It was dangerous to leave it so high for that long.

I called in a nephrologist, and we connected her to a dialysis machine that could remove the alcohol from her blood stream. Within twenty-four hours she was awake, alert, and felt fine. When asked about the party, she said she had a great time.

KIDNAPPED

People in the main lobby of the hospital recognized that he was disturbed and moved away from him. One person had enough common sense to call security. He was unkempt and talking to himself, seemingly unaware of those around him. He was carrying a claw hammer. A security guard warily approached him and asked if he could be of assistance. The man said, "Yes, you can. I must talk to Doctor Ladd right now! My wife has been kidnapped by the Mafia and sold into white slavery. Doctor Ladd was probably the last person she saw before she was taken!"

I had known Mrs. Braxton for many years. She was a regular patient at the clinic for herself and her children. She was a nice lady, but she could not be considered physically attractive. She was morbidly obese and always had the smell of sweat about her from the dampness entrapped between the rolls of fat. She had acne and facial hair. In the past year, her problems were mostly related to her husband and her failing marriage.

He had lost his job two years ago because of alcoholism. When his unemployment insurance ran out, he didn't look for another job. He continued to drink at home, alone, and he talked to himself a lot. Isolated as he was, he gradually became very suspicious of her activities. He would question her endlessly about where she had been, whom she saw, what they said, and what they did. Frequently, he called her at work to see if she was there. Recently, she had the feeling that he was following her. I told her that he was probably mentally ill and dangerous. I asked if she could get him to come to see me or a psychiatrist. "Not likely," she said. "It would be easier for me and the kids to just leave and start elsewhere." "Don't you want him to get well again?" I asked. "I don't think he ever was well," she replied.

The telephone operator paged me and asked me to go to the chaplain's office where Mr. Braxton and the chaplain were waiting for me. She also briefed me as to what had happened and told me what to expect. When I arrived, Mr. Braxton still had the hammer in his hand. I told him that we were all safe from the Mafia now because we had a security guard and to please give me the hammer, which he did.

"What's happening, Mr. Braxton?" I asked. "My wife is gone. Her clothes are gone. She must have been kidnapped by the Mafia and sold into white slavery. I thought she had gone to work, but when I called there, they told me that she had never come in. I walked the streets looking for her, and when I couldn't find her, I thought she had gone to see you. But her clothes are gone. The Mafia must have come in when I was out and got her clothes for her."

He had not noticed or didn't care that his children and their clothes were gone too. "I'm so tired," he said. "I have been looking for her for three days and I can't sleep. I need to sleep. I need to shut off my mind." We struck a deal. I would get the police to look for her and get her back, and he would stay at the hospital where we would help him sleep and shut off his mind.

The police found her and the children. She did not want to come back or have anything to do with him. She eventually got a divorce. I would see him from time to time. When he stayed off the alcohol and took his medication, he was all right. When he stopped his medicine, he ended up back in the hospital.

The last time I saw him he said he didn't think that his wife had ever loved him.

THEN AND NOW

I was fortunate to practice during the golden age of medicine. It was during that time that enormous technological and scientific progress was made in the diagnosis and treatment of patients. These advances actually led to a striking increase in life expectancy and a decrease in suffering. Each year produced more miracle drugs, vaccines, and treatment modalities. Diagnostic tools became available that can only be compared to "Star Trek" and "Buck Rogers in the Twenty-First Century." Diseases that were one hundred percent fatal or disabling became readily treatable with excellent results. All of this came with an ever-expanding price tag.

There was little interference in the practice of medicine by big government. Malpractice suits against physicians were uncommon. Physicians and their patients seemed to have a warm personal relationship. They trusted each other and were concerned about each other. I will tell you two stories of "then." You supply your own stories for "now."

Mrs. Harris was in her fifties when she came to the clinic with crampy abdominal pain and occasional blood in her stools. Her general examination was normal except for the pallor of chronic anemia. In the office, we gave her enemas and using a sigmoidoscope, I could see and biopsy a tumor in her colon. The diagnosis was cancer of the colon.

Further testing showed no evidence that the malignancy had spread. One week later the surgeon and I removed the tumor and a large segment of her colon. We were delighted when the pathologist reported that the cancer was confined to the inner lining of the colon and had not penetrated deeply. All of the regional lymph nodes were negative for cancer.

We all felt good because we had a cure. She recovered fairly quickly but complained of pain low in the left side of her abdomen.

At her annual checkup she had no complaints at all. A complete physical exam revealed a mass, low in the left side of her pelvis. Surely it was a recurrence of her cancer. I felt sick to my stomach. I told her I felt a mass and that we would get an x-ray to see if it would clarify what it was.

The film was on the view box and, from across the room, I could see the mass. I was stunned. It clearly was a surgical sponge! It had been inadvertently left in her abdomen at the time of her surgery. I was now relieved for her and anxious for myself and the hospital. Leaving a sponge in the abdomen is inexcusable! I went down the hall and showed the x-ray to the surgeon.

He looked at the film and sucked on his pipe. He was quiet. Then he turned to me and said, "Let's tell her the good news."

Mr. and Mrs. Harris, the surgeon, and myself sat in his consultation room. He showed them the x-ray and said, "See the fuzzy area with the squiggly lines? That is not a recurrence of your cancer. It is a sponge that I left behind when I did your surgery. I'm sorry about that. It is not supposed to happen, but it did. I apologize. It cannot stay there. I will make arrangements for you to be admitted to the hospital, and we will remove it. Needless to say, there will be no charge by myself or the hospital. We are both very sorry about this, but are glad that your cancer did not come back."

There was no anger expressed. There were no threats or accusations, only relief. The surgery to remove the sponge was done the next week. The patient continued to come to our clinic for another twenty-four years until she passed on. That was then. How about now?

Julia and Nels lived by the Des Plaines River. They were in their late seventies and had been married more than fifty years. They had moved into a new house when they were newlyweds. Their children were born there. Now it was an old frame house that still had a wood-burning stove. Indoor plumbing had been added in the thirties. Nels had worked for the same railroad that rattled their windows as it passed by the house.

Their children wanted them to leave the old place and wanted to build them a new house on top of the hill. The old couple refused. "All of our happiness has been in this place, and we will live here until we die."

I never saw either of them at the clinic. They had never bothered with doctors and had always been healthy. Then, one of the daughters called and asked me to see Julia, at home, as she was out of breath.

It was springtime by the river, and I walked on wooden planks over the flooded ground to the front door. Julia had "dropsy" (an old-time word for chronic congestive heart failure).

Her heart was old, damaged, and inefficient. It caused fluid to back up into the venous system. She began to retain fluid, first in her legs. It gradually extended to the level of her groin. It extended up into her abdomen and ballooned out like an advanced pregnancy. Eventually, the fluid began to accumulate in her lungs. If allowed to continue, it would have rapidly led to her death. This scenario is common and is as old as mankind itself. It is also easy to treat.

I gave her digitalis to strengthen her heart and make it work more efficiently. (A very old drug for a very old disease.) I gave an intravenous cocktail of drugs to help her breathe and to diurese away enormous amounts of fluid. I gave her diuretics to take by mouth and minerals to replace the chemicals she was losing. I restricted her salt intake. When I saw her a week later, it was hard to recognize her. She had diuresed away forty-six pounds and felt fine.

Her bill was as follows:

1. Two house calls at $5.00 each $10.00

2. Intravenous medication $ 4.00

3. Oral medication $ 8.50
          ————
          total $22.50
          (1964 dollars)

I told my mentor about the case, and he agreed that treating dropsy was rewarding because the results were so dramatic. He cautioned me that it would come back, and each time it would be more difficult to treat. In ten months time, I was back at the house. Julia was severely short of breath. Her dropsy had come back. We again treated her aggressively and she responded, but she continued to be mildly short of breath.

1. Three house calls $15.00

2. Assorted medication $13.25
          ————
          total $28.25

Eight months later I rushed out to the house, and she was in extremis. She did not respond to treatment and died with her husband's arms around her.

I recently read (1993) that the average survival time after the first episode of congestive heart failure is a year and a half; essentially the same now as then. Julia stayed in her own home with her husband. She stayed out of the hospital and the nursing home. She was not tested and bled ad infinitum. Her total medical cost for one and a half years was less than one hundred dollars. Think about how this scenario would play today!

FRANKENSTEIN'S LAW

The Bible says you cannot be a prophet in your own land. Marketing specialists know that an expert is somebody with a briefcase who is more than fifty miles from home.

In medicine, there is a general feeling that, "It's better elsewhere." Consequently, people with medical concerns in small towns go to larger communities for their medical care. Likewise, people in larger towns go to the "big city" and big city people go to the major medical centers scattered across America. It reaches a level of absurdity when people with no specific complaints will travel hundreds of miles for a general medical evaluation. This brings us to "Frankenstein's Law," which states: "You created this monster. Now you must take care of it."

The phone rings at two o'clock in the morning and a woman says, "I had a hysterectomy done at Ivory Tower Medical Center in Far-Away Place last week, and now I can't pee." My answer is simple. "Call Ivory Tower Medical Center and talk to your doctor." She would then typically reply, "I did. He is not available, and they told me to call a local doctor." My answer is, "No, no, no, no," and then I explain "Frankenstein's Law" to her.

I am not out-and-out cruel to her. But I will not respond to her need. It was created by selecting a distant physician for something that could have been done, just as well, locally. It is not my fault, nor my problem, that her doctor is not available to her. She and her doctor created this problem, and they will have to solve it without me. I am sure that emergency rooms all over the country see these "monsters" all the time.

I have been called callous, irresponsible, sadistic, and a mean-spirited sonofabitch; none of which I take personally! Then, I go back to sleep.

If I respond to these people and the enormous variety of situations they present, I cannot come out right. First, they are not selecting me by choice, but by default. I'm the only one available. If they get a poor result, I'm to blame. After all, "This never would have happened at Ivory Tower Medical Center." Secondly, if they really get a bad result because of the nature of the case and/or the inadequacy of the surgeon, then I, too, am named in the malpractice suit simply because I saw the patient. Lastly, I do not get paid if I respond to their problem because of "global fees." The insurance company says, "Hey, we paid the surgeon for total care, and he should have provided that service." The patient, when billed, replies, "My insurance company will take care of it."

Previously, I had explained to you the concept of physician and patient being bonded together. I will do everything I can for *my* patient. Other than life-threatening emergencies, I have no need or obligation to respond to other doctors' patients and problems.

LOVE

"Joy" was inappropriately named, as she was very quiet and withdrawn. I saw her for the first time when she was a twenty-two-year-old married woman who was three months pregnant.

My routine for pregnancy care started with a complete history and physical examination of the patient. Thereafter, she would be examined monthly until her eighth month, every two weeks into her ninth month, and then once a week until her delivery.

During the initial exam, I became concerned about Joy's mental health. It was as if she were in neutral. She was not sad, nor was she happy. She asked no questions and only spoke in response to questions. She was introverted and lacked spontaneity, but I could not say she was mentally ill. She apparently functioned well in her own home, had a job at a factory, and slept well at night. This pattern continued through her entire pregnancy. I asked her to bring her husband with her for some of the prenatal visits, but he never came. I asked her how her marriage was, and she replied, "OK."

Her delivery day finally came, and she delivered a little girl with no physical problems or complications. Her husband was not there for her labor or delivery, nor did he ever come to the hospital to see the child. On the morning after the delivery, Joy asked me to arrange for a private adoption.

I asked her if she had a husband. She told me she did and that he had told her that she could not come home with the baby. I asked her if the little girl was his child, and she assured me that she was. "There are other options," I said. "You can make it on your own. We can arrange counseling for you and your husband and work it out." She shook her head and said, "He won't come for counseling, and I can't live without him." "This whole thing is crazy," I said. "Before you do anything, let me have a psychiatrist come talk with you. Let me get the hospital social service involved. There has to be a way to help you! Do you want to keep this baby?" "Oh, I do," she said, "But I can't."

When all was said and done, the baby went out for adoption. I saw her husband for the first time when he came to take her home. He told me to mind my own business and would not talk with me.

Almost every new mother has a period of depression during the two weeks after delivery. It is usually short-lived and self-limiting and clears without treatment. Joy's depth of depression was monumental. She was unable to sleep, could barely eat, and wept constantly. She hardly spoke and, when she did, she spoke of death and dying. I admitted her to the psychiatric unit under the care of the psychiatrist that saw her after her delivery.

For depressed people, the road back to happiness or contentment is long and hard. Joy never made it all the way back. She continued in her marriage and eventually returned to her job at the factory. I saw her at the clinic about once a year. Her depression continued. She never laughed, and I never saw a spontaneous smile. Neither medication nor psychotherapy helped. Periodically she would require a psychiatric hospitalization.

She was thirty-seven years old when she died by her own hand. Her husband had left her, and she could not live without him.

What is this thing called love?

UNDERSTANDING

She wept silently and rocked back and forth in her chair. She was a thin, pale woman in a flowered print dress. A lacy decorative handkerchief was folded into a design and pinned to her dress over her left breast. Her hair was pulled back tightly into a bun at the back of her head. Around her neck she wore a cross carved out of a piece of walnut from her native Appalachia.

She leaned forward and said, "I'm not sick. I need to talk to someone about my daughter. She is twenty-two years old and has moved out of our house into an apartment." "It's not unusual for a twenty-two-year-old to leave home and get her own place," I answered. "But, you don't understand. She has moved in with a man, and I didn't raise her to behave that way," she said with much righteous indignation. "That's not unusual either. It's really beyond your control. She is twenty-two years old." She went on with, "You don't understand. This man has been married before and has only recently been divorced." I said, "You can't hold his previous failed marriage against him. He's entitled to a new start. He is not married now, and your

108

daughter has selected him." "You don't understand," she said again. "He has three children from his previous marriage." "I understand that. Your daughter knows about the children, and she still wants him. He can't throw them away."

"You don't understand anything. He doesn't even have a job." "Your daughter won't stay with him if he's not the right person!" I replied.

She stood up and put her face in mine and said, "He's black."

"I'm sorry," I said. I didn't understand.

TEN PERCENT

I learned in the military that ten percent never get the word. No matter what you do to disseminate information, ten percent never get the message and remain ignorant about something important. Replacement parts for military hardware are often designed with nonfunctional knurls and flanges so that they cannot possibly be installed incorrectly and still fit the proper place. But "the ten percent" get the job done by filing off the knurl or cutting off the flange and thereby create catastrophe.

The O.S.H.A. (Occupational Safety and Health Administration) is battling that ten percent continuously. They have produced reams of printed information covering every industry and every occupation in an effort to protect workers from hazard and injury. Some of it is silly, such as explaining to dairy farmers that wet cow manure is slippery. Some of it seems to be excessive as when giving contractors specifications for building a fence around a construction site.

They are trying to teach common sense, which cannot be taught. Ten percent of our population does not have common sense. The ten percent is probably equally divided between labor and management.

Our Town has a small industrial base consisting of oil refineries, a steel mill, and small factories. All of them also produce injury.

There was a chemical company just outside of town that had a huge mixing machine. It was a steel structure, two stories high and totally open to the weather. The heart of the machine was a large holding vat with three large interlocking mixing paddles. It was similar to a kitchen mixing machine, and it basically did the same thing on an enormous scale. Different dry chemicals came up conveyor belts and fed into the vat where they were crushed together and thoroughly mixed. The mixture then drained out the bottom through a chute for commercial processing. The machine could be run twenty-four hours a day by one operator standing on the metal catwalk, the mixing paddles at his feet.

There had been a freezing rain all night long. The streets and trees were glazed with a quarter inch of ice. The fire department called at ten a.m. There had been a fatal accident at the mixing machine. They wanted me to come out and pronounce the victim dead. I drove out to the site and spoke with the fireman in charge. "Where is the body"? I asked. "Up there," was the reply. "You get there by climbing up this ladder." It was a metal ladder and completely encased in ice. A fireman lowered a harness from above, and I climbed up the ladder, secure in the harness. The catwalk was totally glazed. I could hardly stand. The open maw of the mixing vat was at my feet. There was no guardrail, nothing to hold on to. The only safety device was an ordinary clothesline strung across the vat. It was connected to a shutoff switch. If you fell into the vat, you were supposed to catch the clothesline to turn off the machine. There were two legs sticking up between the paddles and one boot was floating on the surface.

Occupational deaths and injury are preventable. Men are killed falling off roofs because of no protection. Men are buried alive when trenches cave in. They are killed in explosions and fires. Trucks back over them. They are asphyxiated in underground tunnels and tanks. They are electrocuted. They are crushed. It's all preventable!

How do we reach the ten percent? I don't know. Can O.S.H.A. help? I don't know.

EXPECTATIONS

Patients have no way of knowing whether they are receiving good medical care or not. What they do have is a perception that they are happy or unhappy with their care based on their preconceived expectations. If the physician and his treatment of their illness meet their expectations, patients will believe they have received good medical care. If the physician does not meet their expectations, they will be unhappy and believe they have received poor care.

Some physicians are quite skilled in meeting the patient's expectations, and the patients love them. Nevertheless, they may practice poor and inappropriate medicine. Some physicians practice excellent technical medicine and have no skills in responding to the patients' expectations. Consequently, they do not have successful practices. In the old days, this skill was referred to as a "bedside manner."

Jeff

Jeff Clark came to my office for a second opinion. His doctor, who had been his physician for twenty years and in whom he had great faith, had recommended that he have surgery to cure his duodenal ulcer. However, his friends and family, who did not use that physician, suggested that he get a second opinion. I was a new doctor in town and had no reputation one way or another. Thus, he came to my office.

The patient revealed a ten-year history of intermittent heartburn, relieved by antacids and aggravated by certain foods and overindulgences. His weight had been relatively constant. He had no vomiting, and his ulcer had never bled or perforated. I asked why his doctor had recommended surgery for him and was told, "To prevent complications." His physical examination was normal. I ordered x-rays of his upper G.I. tract, which were normal and showed no evidence of an ulcer, past or present.

I met with him and explained that he needed no surgery. His heartburn could be controlled by diet and antacids. He thanked me for my help and left.

I was really pleased with myself. I had saved him from an unnecessary operation. I had a great future here. I was really smug until I saw his name on the surgical schedule.

Danny

Danny Smart was an energetic eight-year-old whom I saw fairly often for a variety of complaints. In six months I saw him several times for abdominal pain. His mother was very concerned that he might have appendicitis.

I examined him and explained to her that there was no evidence on physical examination or anything in the tests that we had done to suggest appendicitis. I treated him symptomatically and "expectantly." Each time he recovered in twenty-four hours.

On the fateful day, he again presented with abdominal pain. His mother again said, "He really should have his appendix out." His examination was normal. I recommended that we treat him as before and told her to call back in the afternoon if he were still having symptoms. I did not hear from her, and I assumed all was well.

Three days later I received a letter from Mrs. Smart, which basically stated that I was an incompetent sonofabitch. She had brought her son to a surgeon who immediately took him to the operating room and removed his appendix "just in time, before it burst." I was lucky that she was not going to sue me, but she would tell all her friends and neighbors how incompetent I was. I could hardly believe it. I was really upset that she had not called back when Danny had continued to be ill.

A week later, while doing my charts in medical records, I pulled the chart on Danny Smart. The pathology report clearly stated that the surgeon had removed a normal appendix.

Elvera

Elvera Stark had been my patient for many years, and we got along well. She had always been in good health, but now at seventy, she began to have vascular problems. She could walk about one hundred yards and would then have to stop because of severe pain in her left leg. Evaluation by a vascular surgeon revealed a complete occlusion of her left femoral artery. This could be helped by having an operation that would bypass the obstructed artery. The consulting vascular surgeon had done many of these procedures and was quite skilled.

We met with Mrs. Stark and her two daughters from the city. We outlined our treatment program. Both daughters said that no local surgeon was going to operate on their mother and especially in a local "rinky-dink" hospital. They were going to take mama to "Ivory Tower University Hospital" where they knew what they were doing.

Several months later I met one of the daughters at the supermarket where she was shopping for her mother. I asked her how mama was doing and the reply was, "Wonderful. After the operation the leg turned black and had to be amputated. Four days later, she had a massive heart attack. She's home now. Thank God she was at Ivory Tower Hospital."

PETUNIA

It was fourteen below zero, eleven o'clock at night, and the phone rang. It was Fremont Pearce calling to tell me that his wife had fever and chills. I told him to give her some aspirin and that I would see her at nine o'clock in the morning. He said, "Doc, she really looks bad; you better come now." I told him to bring her to the clinic, and I would meet them there. He said, "Doc, there ain't no sense in all three of us going out in the cold. Why don't you just put on your pants and come out to the farm." I couldn't argue with such good logic, so I put on my pants.

Mrs. Pearce appeared to have the flu, and I gave her some medication to help her. Fremont had the coffee on and suggested coffee and pie before I went back out into the cold.

We sat in the kitchen, which was warm and cozy. The frosted windows completely shut out the rest of the world. Under the kitchen table lay a three-hundred-pound sow. I said, "Fremont, there is a big pig under the table." He replied, "Pay no attention to her or she will pester you to death. Her name is Petunia and she loves pie."

117

"She was the runt of the litter. I knew I was supposed to leave her with the others, and she would either make it or not, but I couldn't do it. She was so darned cute; I brought her in and bottle-fed her. That was years ago. We became buddies. She's smarter than any dog I ever had. Look how clean and pretty she is. She's housebroke and does tricks too."

On command, the huge porker sat up and begged for pie. "Sit" and "Roll over," produced spectacular performances. The *pièce de résistance* was "play dead," whereupon she lay on her back with her legs folded across her body.

It was absolutely unreal. It was midnight, below zero in January, and I was in a farm kitchen in Illinois watching a pig do tricks.

Medical school never said a thing about this.

SOUL SEARCHING

It's easy to write about triumphs and successes. Everyone likes to think of himself as a winner. But what about the disasters: the poor results, the missed diagnoses, the deaths? Could I have done better? If a similar situation presented itself, would I treat it differently? Could the catastrophe have been avoided? I don't know. If someone else had treated the patient, would the results have been different? I don't know.

In thirty years of practice, I have had my share of patient catastrophes — my share of sleepless nights, anguish, and depression. Three cases still haunt me after all these years.

Karen

Karen was twenty-six years old and this was her third pregnancy. There was a four-year-old and an eighteen-month-old at home. It was an easy delivery, fast and uncomplicated. The baby was just fine. Everybody was happy.

119

In those days, patients usually stayed in the hospital three days after a delivery. Karen was up and around and had no complaints. I saw and checked her each morning, and all was well. On the last day, she complained of discomfort in her left hip. I examined her hip, abdomen, and leg and could find nothing wrong. She walked well, without a limp. I assumed her discomfort was from being on the delivery table. Perhaps her thighs had been spread too wide. It was not a significant pain.

I wrote orders to discharge her home and asked her to see me in ten days. While getting dressed to go home, she suddenly collapsed and died.

The autopsy revealed an enormous blood clot in her lungs. It had formed in the pelvic veins on the left side. While getting dressed, the clot had come loose and carried by the venous flow, traveled to her chest, instantly killing her.

Three babies without a mother! It was heartbreaking. I was their doctor as they grew up. Every time I saw them, I saw their mother and wondered what could I have done.

Ralph

Ralph Carlson was a new patient. He was sixty-seven years old and he was charming. He could have been in television commercials as everyone's grandfather. He had a warm friendly smile, and his eyes twinkled behind his Ben Franklin glasses. You couldn't help but like him!

One week earlier something happened to him. He was visiting and talking with his daughter. Suddenly his speech became garbled and unintelligible. His right arm and leg wouldn't work. He sat down to avoid falling.

Within an hour he had completely recovered with no residual signs or symptoms. He wanted to dismiss the episode as a "spell," but his daughter insisted that he see a doctor.

Other than the present illness, he had been in good health all of his life. He took no medication. "This is a lot of fuss over nothing," he told me. However, examination of his neck revealed a high-pitched whistling sound over his left carotid artery. Special x-rays of the arteries of his neck clearly showed that his left carotid artery was over ninety percent obstructed with an ulcerated fatty plaque. Only a small trickle of blood flowed through.

What had happened to Mr. Carlson was that a clot had formed on the ulcerated plaque. It broke off and traveled to his brain, causing a little stroke. Untreated it would happen again. Eventually, it would block the artery completely and produce a massive stroke.

This finding was good news. He had no permanent damage. The fatty obstruction could be surgically removed. After recovery from surgery he would be fine and not at risk for stroke. He saw a vascular surgeon and the surgery was scheduled.

The surgery went very well. The artery, from the outside, looked like it was plugged with dirty wax. We put in a special bypass tube so blood could freely flow around the obstruction and oxygenate his brain while we operated on the obstructed artery. We opened up the artery and dissected out the fatty, rubbery plug. The artery was now clean and shiny inside. We repaired the artery and removed the bypass tube. The blood literally rushed through the now nonobstructed artery to his brain. We felt good. This beautiful bit of surgery had saved him from a major stroke.

We moved him from the operating room to the recovery room. He woke up and was able to speak and move his arms and legs. He sleepily told me again, "This is a lot of fuss over nothing."

Two hours later, while still in the recovery room, he had several convulsions and became unconscious. The surgeon and I rushed back to the recovery room, but there was nothing we could do. He had suffered a major stroke.

He did not die. He did not recover. He was unable to speak and unable to walk. His right arm and leg were totally paralyzed and useless. There was no warm and friendly smile. There was no twinkle in his eye, only frustration and anger.

I took care of him at the nursing home for several years. I told him how sorry I was and asked him for some sign of forgiveness. It was not given. The anger and frustration stayed with both of us. Seeing him each time was like doing penance.

Cheryl

Cheryl was a senior in college. I had known her for most of her life. Her family had been coming to the clinic for many years. She had returned to Our Town for the Christmas break and made an appointment to see me.

She told me, "Something is wrong. For two months I have had constant pain in my right side. It gets worse when I eat, and I have lost twenty pounds. I don't feel good."

A complete physical examination revealed a large tender mass in the right side of her pelvis. The mass was hard, heavy, and very tender. It was serious trouble. I had hoped it would be an ovarian cyst, but feared that it would be an ovarian cancer. Special tests and studies were done, which demonstrated the problem was not ovarian at all. Cheryl had Crohn's Disease.

This was certainly a better diagnosis than ovarian cancer, but it was still not good. Crohn's Disease is a localized inflammation of the bowel of unknown cause. It is a chronic condition that has periodic flare-ups. Areas of bowel become inflamed and develop ulcerations that can perforate into the abdominal cavity to produce peritonitis and abscess. It is a slowly progressive disease and often produces a lifetime of illness with recurrent hospitalizations and multiple surgical procedures.

I referred her to a specialist in Crohn's Disease. He treated her with various medication in an attempt to improve her condition and avoid surgery. However, she continued to be ill, the mass persisted, and she developed signs of bowel obstruction. The surgeon and myself had also been following her. The three of us concurred that it was time to intervene surgically.

At the time of surgery, we found that the disease was confined to the very end of the small bowel. It was almost completely obstructed, markedly swollen, and had perforated to form a pelvic abscess. The surgery was long and tedious. The abscess was drained. The segment of diseased bowel was removed, and the small bowel was reconnected.

We were pleased. She had no other areas of active Crohn's Disease. The surgery went well. We felt we had done her a service. She would be fine.

She was not fine. In the recovery room, surrounded by doctors, specialty nurses, and high-tech equipment, she died. Her blood pressure fell; she stayed in shock and slipped away, out of this world, with everyone frantically trying to bring her back.

The autopsy did not demonstrate the cause of her death. This was a totally unexpected and unexplained surgical death. Grand rounds were held, and the case was presented in great detail to the medical staff. After extensive discussion, we still had no explanation and did not know what we could have done differently.

The surgeon, the gastroenterologist, and I met with the family. We talked about all that had happened since Cheryl had come to the clinic. We reviewed the charts, our thoughts, and the autopsy report. We held each other and wept.

There is an old saw that says, "Doctors bury their mistakes." These are buried in my mind. I don't know what the mistakes were, but they refuse to stay buried. They come to the surface from time to time and cause sadness, soul searching, and pain.

OFFICE CALLS

Almost every day something happened in my office that made me smile, laugh, or sweat. Many of them stuck in my memory.

Moment of Truth

Vasectomy has always been a good, safe, simple office procedure to produce sterility. For many years I did one or two each week. To ensure its effectiveness, I would get a sperm count six weeks after the procedure. Unfortunately, not everyone came in to get that follow-up sperm count.

He sat in my office with fire in his eyes. He pointed at me and shouted, "You botched my vasectomy. My wife is pregnant and I'm going to sue your ass."

I quickly skimmed through his chart. I had done the vasectomy a year previously and much to my regret, there was no follow-up sperm count. A little sweat appeared on my brow, accompanied by a little nausea and heartburn. "You and I are going to have a moment of truth," I said. "Give me an ejaculate right now, and we will do a sperm count." I left him in the room with his fantasies and a specimen bottle.

Later, we both went to the laboratory and put a sample of the ejaculate under the microscope. There was not a sperm to be seen. I looked at him with sorrow in my eyes and told him, "You are angry at the wrong man."

Cover Yourself

She was a "sweet young thing" and had come in for a complete history and physical exam. I took an extensive history and gave her two towels with the instruction: "Get completely undressed and cover yourself with these towels." I left the room.

When I returned, she was naked, sitting on one towel and had the other wrapped around her hair like a turban. I did not comment. I did the exam and went about my business.

The Last Word

I am firm with little kids. When I examine them or have to do something to them, I do not give them choices. To say to a child, "Would you please open your mouth," implies that he has a choice. Given that choice, he will say, "No!" Far better to say, "Open your mouth," and imply that there is no choice. The same is true of shots. "Count one, two, three with me," and it's done without a fight. Ninety-nine out of one hundred times there is no problem.

But what about the one in a hundred that clamps his mouth shut or bolts away running around the room? That child needs to be immobilized, told what is going to happen, and then, just do it!

I don't think I have emotionally or physically damaged anyone with this approach.

I had just had a tough encounter with a four-year-old boy, and I was walking through the waiting room. He ran up to me and pulled on my pant-leg. I looked down at his angelic tear-streaked face, and he loudly said, with just the right quiver in his voice, "Doctor, doctor, please don't hurt me anymore."

Thank You

The police had subdued him, and he was in restraints. Unfortunately, he was still yelling and thrashing around. He was psychotic and was a danger to himself and others. The police had brought him to the clinic to be sedated and admitted to a psychiatric hospital, which I did.

Four months later, I walked into my examining room, and he was sitting there. He was quite calm. He looked at me and asked, "You the guy that had me locked up in the loony bin?" With much trepidation I said, "I am." He reached into his pocket and I jumped up. I thought, "Here it comes; I'm going to be killed by a mental patient." He pulled out a small package wrapped in decorated green paper. "This is for you, doc. I made it in occupational therapy. I really want to thank you for helping me. I was nuttier than a fruitcake." I opened the package, and it was a handmade tooled leather key case. It still holds my keys today.

Discharge

A standard question during a gynecological exam is, "Do you have any vaginal discharge?" A standard answer is either yes or no.

One matron replied, "If I do, it must be rust."

POWER

Physicians have and use powers of which they are unaware. They have the power of suggestion coming from an authority figure. If the patient has confidence in the physician, whatever treatment he prescribes will be more effective than if it came anonymously. Recent studies have demonstrated repeatedly that placebos (inert pills) have therapeutic effects. I have "bought" warts from children for a nickel, and they have disappeared. My mentor prescribed black aspirin for a variety of complaints with excellent results.

Physicians have the power of laying on hands. Whenever I examined or treated patients, I always had one hand on them as if therapy could be transmitted by touch. Faith healers and charlatans do the same thing. This power of touching goes both ways. People often want to touch the rich and famous as if some of it would rub off on them.

Physicians have the power to command verbally. Just telling patients to stop smoking is totally effective in one out of twenty smokers. This power is shared with the

130

clergy. What believer would argue with the Reverend Billy Graham, the Pope, or Moses!

These powers are very effective in helping people, but can certainly be abused for personal gain. Quackery flourishes in America and utilizes all of these modalities.

CHANCES

Everyone who wants a second chance, gets it. If he needs and wants a third chance, he can have that too.

In my career, I have been an observer of joy and tragedy. The joys we seem to accept as our just due. The tragedies damage us severely, and we must recover over time. The human spirit has enormous capacity to adjust.

We all would like to think that our spouse is our one true love. But what happens when that spouse dies? For the survivor, life must go on. It does not seem to matter whether the couple has been married for one year or fifty years.

The pattern I have seen is that, usually, within a year or two of the loss of a spouse, the survivor introduces me to his or her fiancé, and life begins again for the both of them. I am always delighted when I see that happen. I think it's terrible to be alone and not have the intimacy of two people sharing their joys and sorrows.

Research has been done which shows that survivors, who continue on alone, die at a much earlier age than those who establish a new relationship with another person. From time to time, I have seen the second spouse also die. Then the survivor has to recover again and gets a third chance.

I had a patient who died at age eighty-eight and had outlived three husbands. She also had a boyfriend at the time of her death. She had been married to each of her husbands for almost twenty years. When I pressed her on which one she had loved the most, she said, "The last one, always the last one."

WHAT'S IT WORTH

All my professional career I have heard and read that medical care costs too much and that doctors make too much money. People who say that are usually using their own annual income as the standard to compare.

The media likes to use national averages and usually compares oranges to apples. For example, they may say, "The average physician in America takes home $120,000 a year, which is five times that of the average worker." They never define the "average physician" or the "average worker."

Whenever patients have complained to me about my fees, I have always asked them what they thought my fee should be? Invariably, they are unable to answer the question. Logically, they can't set the fee because they have no idea what the fixed overhead is. However, most of them do agree, whatever the fee is, it's too much! They didn't ask to be sick. They didn't plan on being sick, and they resent paying for it. People buy automobiles and make monthly payments for three or four years because they want the car and are willing to pay for it over time. They don't want to pay the physician because they didn't want the illness.

I would like to try and put things into perspective. When I started in private practice in 1963, my routine office call fee was $4.00. The price of mailing a first class letter was four cents.

In 1993, the routine office call was $32 and the first class letter was twenty-nine cents. Medicare says that my fee is too high and will only pay me $20 for an office visit. I do not hear anyone saying postal workers are overpaid or that the price of postage has exceeded guidelines.

I would like to be paid as if I were a heavy equipment operator who owns his own machine. A large "Case" earth mover costs about $140,000. Not counting residency training, an M.D. degree costs about the same. So we both have the same initial investment.

The machine and the operator can be rented for $150 per hour. Considering all the work the man and his machine can do in changing the face of the earth quickly, that's a good deal.

The "average" family doctor works sixty hours a week, forty-eight weeks a year. At $150 per hour, a doctor would earn $432,000 a year. Assuming an overhead cost of 55 percent, the national average for a family physician, the average take-home pay would be $194,400. It isn't happening. The national average for family physicians is $120,000, and compared to the earth-moving industry he is underpaid.

Don't start me on athletes . . . and corporate CEO's . . . and entertainers!

WHO IS OLD?

My mentor was fifty years old, and we had a party for him. I was twenty-nine. I thought he was old, and I told him so. He laughed and told me that I should make a house call at the farm on Orchard Road. Then I would know what old really is!

One day I did that and met the Ford family. The farm was an original homestead, and four siblings lived in the house. There were two brothers and two sisters. The oldest was Luke, who was ninety-three and the youngest was Sarah, who was eighty-two. They had all been born in that same house, had never married, and had worked the farm together since they were children. They still supervised it, and the fields, barns, and animals were all well cared for.

I sat with them in the parlor surrounded by original Victorian furniture. We talked and drank coffee and ate cupcakes fresh from the oven. They told me about themselves and the farm and made me feel welcome.

The farmhouse walls were decorated with many really old photographs. One caught my eye. It showed the old

136

farmhouse on a dirt road with a ragamuffin barefoot kid on the front porch. The picture was taken around 1900. The house appeared almost the same as now. The kid was one of Our Town's most distinguished senior citizens, and the dirt road had become Interstate 55.

These people were alert, sharp, and working. I thought my mentor was old at fifty, but Luke was already forty-three years old on the day my mentor was born.

I think the secret is work. All of the really old people I have met were still working at something at advanced ages. All of the old "retired" nuns at the convent still have assigned jobs and responsibilities.

The oldest man I ever took care of was one hundred and three years old. The last time I saw him, he insisted we walk in his rose garden, which he still tended.

We may become aged, infirm, and frail, but "old" is a state of mind.

COOKBOOK MEDICINE

Quality care is cost-effective. Under pressure from insurance companies and the government, medical specialty organizations are writing "cookbooks." They call them guidelines, or clinical pathways. They are written protocols created by specialty societies, with input from its members, designed to treat various medical conditions in the safest, most efficient, "cost-effective" manner. They are now being utilized by hospitals as part of managed care.

It is probably a good idea. Critics of the program call it cookbook medicine. They don't know what cookbook medicine really is.

Mrs. Marlene Peck came into my office in 1963 with what appeared to be a normal pregnancy. The diagnosis turned out to be choriocarcinoma, which is a wildly malignant cancer, that in 1963 was almost 100 percent fatal in a year's time. It was quite rare, and there was very little experience in treating it.

I referred her to an Ob-Gyn specialist, but he didn't know any more about it than I did. At that time chemotherapy was a new thing, and there were no regional oncology centers to which we could refer her.

We reviewed the literature at the hospital library and found several articles, written in faraway places, reporting success with surgery followed by chemotherapy. The drug recommended was also used in the treatment of leukemia and so it was available to us.

The untreated disease was 100 percent fatal. The chemotherapy required very large doses and had severe complications, including death. We took the article's written protocol and followed it exactly, like a cookbook recipe.

She developed all the side effects. Her hair fell out. Her bone marrow became severely depressed. She bled into her skin because her platelets were gone. She became infected in her lungs and bloodstream because her white blood cell count was so low. She became anemic as her red cells disappeared. She damn near died as we followed the protocol!

That was more than thirty years ago. She is living and well today, and I still see her from time to time.

Cookbook medicine isn't all that bad.

HISTORY, HISTORY, HISTORY!

Every disease has a natural history and a natural course. The events leading up to the onset of the disease and its progression is known as history. The earliest symptoms of the most severe diseases may be mild and unnoticed by the patient, but can be identified and extracted from the patient by the inquiring physician.

When I was a medical student, I had a marvelous teacher who emphasized history — history — history! He taught that the history of the presenting patient was the most important part of a medical evaluation, and that properly done, it would give you the most likely diagnosis before ever doing a physical exam or a laboratory test. He said that the history should give you the probable diagnosis, and that the physical examination and laboratory testing either confirm or deny what you already believe to be true. To prove his point, he would divide his students into groups of two, each to see the patient separately. One student took the history and did not physically examine the patient. The other examined the patient physically, but

140

was not allowed to talk to him. The student taking the history almost always had the correct diagnosis, while the one doing the physical exam hardly ever did.

The style of medical practice used today does not emphasize the physician taking the history directly from the patient, but tends to use forms and even computers rather than the personal exchange between the patient and the doctor. One of the biggest complaints that patients have is, "My doctor doesn't talk to me."

Doctors today seem to overemphasize the laboratory. Unbelievable sums of money are spent on unnecessary lab work and procedures. We seem to have great faith in testing, printed forms, and numerical measurements in general. Under the new managed-care programs, perhaps this can be corrected, but I doubt it.

An important feature of taking a history is that it builds a communication bond between the patient and his doctor. It allows the patients to tell you things about themselves that are highly personal, so that the physician can better understand their problems.

A young woman, whom I knew well, once presented to me and said, "When I have intercourse with my husband, I always bleed." I replied, "Does that mean when you have intercourse with someone else you do not bleed?" She said, "That's right." That allowed us to get into the subject of her failing marriage, which is why she came to the physician in the first place.

Try getting that from a computerized form!

PICK OF THE LITTER

For more than one hundred years, people have discussed and argued about the relative effects of genetics and environment on the development of the individual.

In animal husbandry, there is no dispute or debate. Breeders of quality animals always breed the best they have to the best they can find, whether it's a racehorse for speed, or cattle for muscle mass. Once the genetic product arrives, whatever happens environmentally to that animal, good or bad, will certainly affect whatever standard you are trying to establish or measure. The opposite is not true. If the horse does not have the genetic ability to run fast, no amount of training or conditioning will make him a successful racer.

In a litter of puppies, you can compare a dozen individuals of the same age and parents. Although they all have the same mother and father, they are not genetically identical, due to normal random reproductive variation. But they are certainly more alike than different. Depending on the trait you are looking for, some puppies have more of it and others less. The "pick of the litter" is the puppy that has more of the traits that you particularly want. Once you have selected him and take him home, this genetically unique puppy will be impacted upon by his environment and experience.

What about people? We usually get them one at a time and don't get the pick of the litter. We have to keep whatever genetic package he comes with. After we take the baby home we can impact that infant with environmental experiences, but that is still overlayed on his own genetic material.

I believe, and many pediatricians agree, that newborns seem to have temperamental and personality traits that come with the genetic package. All measurable human traits follow a bell-shaped curve with ninety percent of the individuals being under the bell. They are very similar to each other and, therefore, not unique. The ten percent outside the curve are different and outstanding.

When Maggie was born, she was instantly alert and agitated. She was a healthy newborn but was irritable and intolerant of just about anything that happened to her or around her. In her rages, she would become stiff as a board and red as a beet. When she was one day old, I told her mother she would be a tough one. That baby is now in her late twenties. As a child, she was difficult and headstrong. As a teenager, she was a nightmare. But now she is a mature adult. She has a master's degree in business and is quite successful. She is a very aggressive businesswoman. Her current position reflects the genetic package she came with, influenced by her family, friends, and community. They are all to be commended. They did a good job.

Ruth was a floppy baby, and I worried about her. When she was born, she opened her eyes, looked around, and took a breath. The crying was minimal. As a newborn, she was totally relaxed, and if you held her up in the palm of your hand, she just hung down on all sides like a rag doll. There was nothing wrong with her. She was just relaxed and not irritable. She stayed that way. As a child she was easy to deal with. She never seemed to be a real teenager because she was so calm and rational. She never lost her cool. She is now a kindergarten teacher.

Like water seeking its own level, the genetic package steers us in the direction where we seem to fit best. Hopefully, the environment in which we develop will allow us to do that, rather than forcing the square peg in the round hole.

SKIN-DEEP

Colonel Thomas was a dermatologist in a large military hospital. He was quite competent but had trouble staying focused because he had so much mischief in him. When serious skin problems presented, he was all business. When less than serious problems presented, he was all mischief. He had the need to impress patients. He called ordinary dandruff, "Seborrhea." "That ought to impress them," he said. "Any idiot can diagnose dandruff, but it takes a full colonel dermatologist to diagnose seborrhea." To further impress these "dandruff patients" with his scientific ability, he had them bring in their "hair combings." It was as if he were going to do some exotic testing on these hair samples. It was ludicrous to see a waiting room full of people with little bags of hair combings, all of which ended up in the wastebasket of the workroom. The zenith of his showmanship was reached when he did "the glass test." He simply took an empty water glass, turned it over, and applied the open end to the patient's scalp. He then looked through the bottom of the glass as he moved it around his head. It was the scalp equivalent of a glass-bottomed boat. He would then give them the official diagnosis of seborrhea and prescribe appropriate and effective treatment.

Every now and then a patient would come in with a harmless skin rash that really defied a specific diagnosis. Colonel Thomas was prepared for this too. "Have you ever had this rash before," he would ask. When they confirmed that they had, he would say, "Well, you've got it again." Then he would ask, "How long did it take to go away last time?" When they replied, "four weeks," he would tell them, "It'll probably take six weeks this time." He would then prescribe a harmless soothing lotion, and the patient would depart knowing that they had indeed been diagnosed by a dermatological clinician.

They loved him, and I did too.

About every two years we had a "louse epidemic," in Our Town. It started out with the school nurse sending some kid home with a note saying, "I checked Ricky's hair, and I think he has lice. Please check with your doctor." The thought of her child with lice in his hair is enough to terrorize any suburban housewife. The first question that appears in her mind is, "Where did he get it from? Probably from that Randy Smith." This is immediately followed by a telephone call to Mrs. Blanche Smith. "Blanche, you better check Randy's scalp. I hear there's lice in the school." This scenario was probably repeated a hundred times a week for three to four weeks, and we saw all of those kids, some of them twice. We never saw any lice.

Tattooing is once again becoming popular in America. It used to be a rite of passage for young men going away from home, going to war. Now, just as many women are tattooed as men. These body decorations also made a statement about who you were and what was important to you; "Death Before Dishonor" with a military insignia, "God Bless America" underneath the flag, "Mother" overlayed on a red heart. Sometimes it was a "sweetheart's name" with the addition of "forever." That's the main problem with tattoos. They are forever. The sweetheart may be long gone, but the tattoo is still there. A vulgar tattoo may be on the arm of a man who is a conservative stockbroker or a preacher.

For some reason, tattoos "grow." The person with a tattoo on the right shoulder, soon gets one on the left. It's as if he feels the need to be balanced and symmetrical. Sometimes it's like trying to even up the legs of a wobbly chair. They keep adding to it and never quite get it right. I don't understand people who get whole body tattoos, but it is not uncommon.

When I was a kid, we had "cockamamies." They were tattoo images that you could transfer onto your skin and have a temporary tattoo. You could wash them off or keep them as long as your mother would let you. I could sometimes get them to last a week. They are back now. I have seen them in the stores, and the kids of today love them as we did. At carnivals and fairs, young people have decorations painted on their faces. It is quite attractive, harmless, and washes off.

I always wanted to get a small tattoo of a bird dog pointing a quail. I once got as far as the door to the tattoo parlor before I chickened out. I knew I would be the only physician in America to get hepatitis B from a tattoo needle.

WHO WAS THAT MAN?

We are what we are, wherever we are. A plumber is always a plumber. A mechanic is always a mechanic, and a physician is always a physician. I am sure that a plumber in church hears the sounds of dripping faucets and running toilets over the sounds of the sermon. He wonders why no one fixes it. The auto mechanic hears every odd sound in someone else's car and knows what needs fixing. Whenever I'm with people, I always pick up on abnormal gaits, posture, mood, and appearance. It's automatic and done without premeditation. I have approached strangers and asked if they were all right and have they seen their doctor lately? Sometimes the inquiry is well received, sometimes it's not.

As Our Town began to grow and the farms were replaced by subdivisions, I had fewer and fewer places to train my bird dogs. I also had problems with the increased and faster traffic. I was always afraid a dog would be hit by a car. The bird hunting season in Illinois is very short, and so I had limited opportunity to kill birds over my dogs, which is important in their training. By sheer luck, I saw an advertisement in the local newspaper. "Wanted. Experienced guides with well-trained bird dogs to guide small hunting parties on a private shooting preserve in Oak Brook, Illinois." Was God talking to me or what? I gave them a call and set up an interview for my training partner and myself.

The shooting preserve was beautiful with long hedgerows and stubble fields with scattered feed patches to attract and hold birds. There were hundreds of acres of prime game bird cover. There were no paved roads and the entire area was fenced, dog tight.

We demonstrated our dogs' ability to find and handle game birds to the preserve manager and knocked his socks off. He signed us up on the spot. "You get paid twenty dollars for a morning hunt and twenty dollars for an afternoon. The clients are pretty generous with tipping, and with those dogs you guys will make a fortune. The club also gives you free lunch."

I didn't tell him I was a physician, and my partner didn't tell him he ran an engineering department. We were there to train dogs! We made arrangements to "work" every Wednesday.

It was a terrific training experience. Our dogs pointed thirty pheasant a day and probably did twenty-five retrieves. They became finished, polished performers. The tips were generous and we bought a lot of "dog stuff." We were having such a good time, we couldn't believe anyone would pay us for it.

We took our jobs very seriously. We were very deferential to the clients. We tipped our hats, told them what great shots they were, and referred to everyone as "sir" or "ma'am."

The day finally came when we guided a party of three physicians. They were wearing leather-faced hunting pants and their shooting jackets had recoil pads on the shoulders. They carried fine double-barreled shotguns. As they tramped through the fields following the dogs, they talked "medicine." They couldn't help themselves. No matter where they were, they were still physicians. I don't think two physicians can socialize without talking shop. I'm guilty too, because I began eavesdropping.

Between points and shots, they were discussing a troublesome case. It seems a forty-five-year-old man came to the physician's office complaining of fatigue and shortness of breath. Examination revealed him to be severely anemic. Further testing showed that he had blood in his stool and was anemic secondary to chronic bleeding in his gastrointestinal tract. The physician had done an upper G.I. series and a barium enema and no pathology was demonstrated. He sigmoidoscoped the patient and saw no abnormalities. He then assumed, probably erroneously, that the bleeding must have come from internal hemorrhoids. The patient was put on large doses of iron, and his blood counts returned to normal.

The fact that the doctor was talking about it now, indicated that he was uncomfortable with the diagnosis and was afraid that he had missed something more important. This all came to me in bits and pieces between shots over a three-hour hunt. By then I was very uncomfortable, because I felt I really needed to tell him what should be done.

We finished the hunt and returned to the clubhouse where the doctors changed their clothes and switched from boots to shoes. At the tailgate of his station wagon I tipped my hat and gave him his game bag full of birds. He gave me ten dollars and said, "It was a great day. Your dogs are something else." I said, "Thank you, sir. By the way, your patient with the blood in his stools probably has a malignancy in his stomach or colon. He needs to be sent to a gastroenterologist in Chicago where he can have a gastroscopy and a long flexible colonoscopy done. That's a new technology that hasn't made it out here yet." With that said, I turned and walked away, with my dog at heel, and never looked back.

In my mind I could hear, "Who was that man? I don't know, but he left a silver shotgun shell!"

FATHERHOOD

Fatherhood is "in." Real men do take care of and relate to their children. Bookstores sell a great variety of "how to" books teaching men parenting skills. Last year at a picnic, I observed several young men. Each held a baby straddling his left hip. Each held a cold beer in his right hand. They were not talking sports or politics, but were discussing child care. "Maria crawls all over the house, and we had to kid-proof it." "Matthew goes to preschool, and it's good for all of us." "Allison eats with a spoon, and it's a mess."

Male athletes and celebrities are photographed with their children. Men are demanding and getting custody rights in divorce cases. Men from chaotic backgrounds who discover they have a child they were unaware of, are going through the courts demanding that the child be given up to them. The wild oats are becoming domesticated.

John Wright could have been "Father Of The Year." When I first met him, he proudly showed me pictures of his children, two boys ages five and seven and a little girl just turned two. They were adorable like all children of that age. He couldn't stop talking about them. I finally had to say, "Mr. Wright, stop. You are here about a medical problem, and that's what we have to talk about."

I saw John about once a year, and each time we went through new pictures, new stories, and updating about his children. The oldest was playing baseball. The second son was starting school. The little girl was taking dance lessons at "Shirley's School of the Dance." This was accompanied by a picture of her in a ballet costume where she was dancing the role of "popcorn." I'll confess. I liked John and I enjoyed hearing about his children. His love for them was unconditional, and he was totally devoted to them. He never missed a little league game, a P.T.A. meeting, or a dance recital. He was always in the background of their activities.

As the years went by, the activities changed. The boys were in Cub Scouts, and he was at the "Blue and Gold Banquets," which is a nightmarish experience of total chaos. He was also at the father-daughter events. These kids were not sent to summer camps. He and his wife, Fran, took them on vacations with them. They were a stable family, and he was a caring, nurturing, loving father.

He was constantly planning for the future. When the oldest started high school, he took a second job. After all, "Colleges cost money." All of them did go to college, and it was a triumph for John who never had that opportunity.

I saw him in the office and received my annual briefing when the boys were away at college. He wasn't his usual self. He lacked the flair and fire he usually had. He seemed to be depressed. We talked about it, and he volunteered that he missed his sons terribly and that his life just wasn't the same when they were away. His daughter was now a teenager and was caught up in girl activities that seemed to exclude him. He said, "It's a good thing I have a second job or I would have a lot of time on my hands."

He came into the office shortly after Christmas. He was feeling good. The family had been together for the holidays, and it was like old times. He then said, "My children are so marvelous, I have decided to become a sperm donor. I want you to make arrangements for me to do that." I burst our laughing, and he rebuked me with, "Don't laugh, I'm serious about this." I said, "John, your kids are great kids, but they are not the be-all and end-all of children. Your genetic pool is not much different from anybody else of West European descent. Furthermore, your genes account for only half of their genetic makeup. Your wife contributed the other half, which I suspect is where they get all their good qualities." He sort of pouted and petulantly said, "I'm serious about this. I want to be a sperm donor." "John. There are plenty of sperm donors out there. They don't need yours. Does this have anything to do with your depression?" He said, "No. My kids are great, and I think society as a whole would benefit if I donated sperm." I said, "Your kids are great because of the way you and your wife raised them, not because of your genes. Besides, selective breeding of people in the United States went out with slavery." He got a little testy and said, "I don't want to talk about it anymore. I brought you a fresh sperm sample. I want you to test it and refer me to a clinic that does artificial insemination." I told him, "I don't need the sample. I will find a fertility clinic that does artificial insemination, and you can deal directly with them. I'll call you when I find one." He thanked me and left.

Unbeknown to me, he left the sperm sample in a properly labeled collection container on my desk. My nurse saw it, assumed it was supposed to go to the lab, and sent it in. The lab thought it was a post-vasectomy specimen and did a sperm count. The report I received the next day stated that there were no sperm whatsoever in the specimen. John was not the biological father of his children! I called Mrs. Wright and asked her to come in and talk.

I really did not know this woman. I had not delivered any of the children, and I saw her only when she brought the kids in for the usual childhood medical problems. She had never been my patient.

She was totally unaware of her husband's plan to be a sperm donor. Her eyes got wide with horror as the story unfolded. The tears began to flow as she read the laboratory report.

She sat, weeping quietly, and then composed herself. There was an awkward silence and then she said, "Do not judge me. Hear me out. I love my husband dearly and in my heart I have never been unfaithful to him. When I was a teenager, I had a baby and put him up for adoption. John knows about that. It was four years after that when I met

John and we married. He wanted children right away and I said fine. It should have been easy. But after more than a year, I still wasn't pregnant. I knew it had to be him because I knew I was fertile. I went to the library and read about infertility and what could be done to overcome it. The whole thing frightened me. I didn't want to go through all those tests and procedures. We didn't have much money, and it would cost a fortune. Not only that, but John thought of himself as a stud. Finding out that he was sterile would really hurt him. So I decided to get pregnant by someone else. John would never know, and we would have the children that we wanted."

I am not a prude, but I couldn't believe what I was hearing. I asked, "How do you go about finding someone to impregnate you? Do you pick someone out and just ask him?" Her eyes flashed with anger. "I am not a stupid woman. I needed someone I knew and was comfortable with. I needed someone who would understand the situation and be discrete. I needed someone who looked like my husband. I used his brother. All of the pregnancies were planned, and there was no passion involved. In fact, it was quite mechanical."

We both sat quietly. I finally found my voice and asked, "What are you going to do?" "I can handle it," she replied. "I will tell him you called about an infertility clinic where he might be a sperm donor. I will tell him that I do not approve, and that I absolutely do not want him to be a sperm donor. We do have three wonderful children. Let someone else do it."

John continued to be my patient and never mentioned the subject again. The children finished college and married and had children of their own. Whenever I saw him, he showed me pictures of his grandchildren and told me how wonderful they were.

I never saw Mrs. Wright again.

John died several years ago. The funeral was well-attended. The pastor dwelled on what a wonderful father and grandfather he had been.

I recently read in the newspaper about a woman who was impregnated by her brother-in-law's sperm delivered via a turkey baster by her loving sister.

It is a wise child that knows his own father.

SHAKES AND SNAKES

"Big Red" had been my patient for years. Although he was an alcoholic, I liked him and we were friends. What I liked best about him was that he had no guile. He was a leveler and told it the way it was. He made no excuses for his drinking and was a hard-working, productive citizen. He had several scrapes with the law for "driving under the influence," but had never had an accident related to alcohol.

Coming home from work, sober as a deacon, he got broadsided on the passenger side by a car that ran a stop sign. He was thrown out of the car, broke his ankle, and generally beat up and skinned his body. He was admitted to the hospital under my care.

His injuries were not severe. But I knew he would go into "D.T.'s," which commonly occurs after alcoholics are injured. The general public thinks of "D.T.'s," humorously, as seeing pink elephants and getting the shakes. It is far more serious than that. It is a horrific illness. The patient with delirium tremens is totally out of his mind, violent, dangerous, and hallucinates snakes, insects, and rodents.

He gets severe tremors and high fever. It lasts three to five days, and if the patient survives, he makes a complete recovery. It has a mortality rate of seven deaths per one hundred cases. (That is much higher than the mortality rate of open heart surgery.) Contrary to popular thought, giving alcohol does not prevent the delirium. However, there are medications that, if started early enough, can prevent some of the cases from occurring.

It was a lovely spring day. Red's room was adjacent to the construction site of a new addition to the hospital. There was a deep excavation just outside his open window, and he could watch the workers. He was in a room full of sunshine and spring flowers. "Looks like a mortuary," he grumbled. "Can I go home?" He was a mess. His abraded skin was covered with bulky dressings making him look like a mummy. His eyes were puffed up, and he peered out from slits. His leg was elevated on a pillow. I had set and cast his ankle fracture the night before. I told him that he had to stay put for a couple of days, and I told him about "D.T.'s." (I had already started medication.) "You have to tell someone if you start to feel shaky or start to see things that aren't quite right." He laughed and said, "Hell, I'm shaky all the time anyhow. As for seeing things that aren't quite right, doesn't it look and feel like this building is tilting and leaning toward that big hole outside the window?" I looked at it, and I did have the feeling that the room was tilted toward the hole. Then he said, "There were also two snakes in here this morning." Well, that did it for me. I medicated the hell out of him.

I called the hospital several times that day, and they reported he was quiet and resting. The next morning I asked him how he felt, and he said, "Tired." I asked, "Have you seen any more snakes?" "What's the matter with you," he said. "I told you yesterday I saw two snakes." I said, "Red, they are not real. They are in your imagination." "They look pretty real to me," he said and reached into his bedside drawer and threw two live garter snakes at me that had crawled through the window from the construction site.

He recovered from the accident. He continued to be an alcoholic. Many years later, he was hit and killed by a speeding car in front of his house. He had not been drinking that day either.

RHYTHM

One of the advantages of practicing family medicine in a Catholic community is the birth rate. Our Town, in years past, had an astronomical birth rate, with much of it being repeat performances by the same women. Large families were the rule. In recent years, the power of the Church to control women's reproductivity has markedly diminished. Now our birth rate is the same as the national average.

Previously, young women planning to marry would make an appointment to discuss the rhythm method of contraception. Now, most young women are using far more reliable methods of contraception long before they marry.

Margaret presented herself at the clinic when she was nineteen. She had graduated from an all-girl Catholic high school a year previously and was working as a bookkeeper. She was planning to marry in three months and wanted to learn about "rhythm." She explained to me, with great sincerity, "The rhythm method is acceptable in the Church and it's natural." I explained to her that it was also quite natural to be pregnant, and that she would probably find herself in that state in less than a year. Couples who diligently follow all the rules of the method still have a high pregnancy rate. I told her, "A newlywed couple probably could not use such a method effectively or happily." She laughed good-naturedly and said, "Whatever happens, happens."

It did "happen." We delivered a little girl, and everyone was very happy.

At her six-week check up, I brought up the subject of birth control. She said that this time she and Rick were really going to use the rhythm method, and it would work.

We delivered another girl fourteen months later. She was not too happy with two children in diapers, but she could manage. Her mother who lived in town would help.

At the six-week checkup, I suggested another method of contraception and she snapped at me, "Doctor, I am a good Catholic woman. I can use the rhythm method and Rick will just have to adjust to it." The third girl was delivered thirteen months later.

All five of them were there for the six-week checkup; three little girls, Rick and Margaret. Our conversation was very brief. "What's it going to be, Margaret," I asked. "No problem," she said. "I'm still a strict observant Catholic. If Rick ever wants to get into bed with me again, he had better get a vasectomy." "No problem," said Rick, "I never was that good a Catholic anyhow."

YOU CALL, WE HAUL

Cars have never been important to me. My goal was always to have reliable transportation to get me from point A to point B. When I first moved to Our Town, I bought a pickup truck. My wife had the family car, and I used the pickup truck. I had it fitted with a spotlight so I could find addresses and mailboxes at night.

I used it all the time in the practice, including going to the clinic and the hospital. In the toughest winters it always started. I never got stuck. I carried three hundred pounds of dry dog food in the bed for additional weight and traction. If I did get stuck in the snow, dry dog food under the wheels gave good traction and out I came. It was ecologically sound too, as the birds ate the scattered dog food and nothing was left but snow. I guess if I really got stuck, I could have eaten the dog food as well.

The truck became my personal trademark. I had one for the entire time I practiced in the country. I was making a statement. I was a country doctor. I had the doors lettered: "Barry Ladd and Sons." At the hospital I took a good-natured ribbing from the doctors who wanted to

163

know if I was a medical doctor or a veterinarian. I took a perverse pleasure in parking it alongside the Cadillacs and Mercedes in the doctors' parking lot.

I was making a house call in a nearby blue-collar town, and as I drove down the neat streets of the subdivision, I noticed almost every driveway had a pickup truck in it, in running condition or otherwise. I laughed inwardly and thought, "When in Rome, do as the Romans do." The man of the house echoed that thought as he came up to me in the driveway and extended his hand with, "Doc, you're one of us." That did not hurt my practice.

I ran my trucks until they literally fell apart. I got an average of one hundred and ten thousand miles out of each one. At that time you could buy four pickup trucks for the price of one Mercedes.

Getting out of the truck at Mrs. Monroe's house, I slammed the door a little too hard and it fell off in her driveway. (I had been meaning to get it fixed.) I picked it up and put it in the bed of the truck. She stood there shaking her head and said, "Doctor Ladd, you need to raise your fees and buy yourself a new truck." One week later I sent her a postcard telling her that I had taken her advice.

The best thing about pickup trucks is that they are totally utilitarian. You can just about go anywhere with them, and the visibility from the high cab is terrific. A Commonwealth Edison lineman was on a power pole in the bottomland along the river. He fell off into the swamp and hit the only large rock in the area, shattering his hip.

His co-worker ran a half mile on a muddy stump-filled access road to get help. At that time paramedics did not exist, and the local mortician ran the ambulance service. (The same vehicle that took you to the hospital might also take you to your grave.) The ambulance was basically a low-slung, soft-sprung Cadillac hearse. There was no way it could get to the accident site. We took the litter from the ambulance and put it in the bed of the pickup truck. With the truck in four wheel drive, we got in and out with the patient in a matter of minutes.

"You call, we haul."

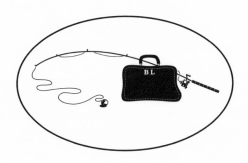

SECRETS

Every family has secrets. They are closely held in the family and are only disclosed under extraordinary circumstances. Think into your own life and family and most of you will find that you too have secrets, not for public scrutiny. The computerized information highway, the media, and the freedom of information act make it harder and harder to keep secrets. That is why politicians and political appointees have had so much difficulty in recent years. It's hard to find anyone who is pristine without at least one skeleton in the closet.

Mr. and Mrs. King appeared to be the all-American family. He had a good blue-collar job. She was a homemaker, and they had two young adult children. They owned their own home. They attended church regularly. Everybody liked them, and they had a large circle of friends and activities. The older son went away to college. After the daughter finished high school she married, and she and her husband moved to Missouri.

Shortly thereafter, Mrs. King, who was chronically ill, developed a malignancy, which led to her death three years later.

Mr. King was alone for about one year and then began dating and socializing again. He was fifty years old, but dated women in their mid-twenties. The general attitude of his friends, especially the men, was "more power to him." Much to everyone's surprise, he married one of the young women.

About six months after they married, he and his bride came to the clinic for complete physical exams. Everything was fine, and they asked me to fill out State of Illinois forms enabling them to take a ten-year-old girl into their home as a foster child. He joked with me and said, "I'm too old to start one from scratch, and a ten-year-old fits better into our lifestyle."

I filled out the forms and was happy to do so. They could really help this young girl. Where the form asked if I had any negative information regarding the applicants, I replied, "No." Where it asked if I recommended this place-ment without reservation, I replied, "Yes."

Two weeks later, Mr. King's married daughter and her husband came to see me. They had made a special trip from Missouri, just to talk with me. The couple sat in the office, but she did all the talking.

"My brother called me and said that my father and his wife are taking in a ten-year-old girl as a foster child. You do not really know my father. From the time I was eleven years old, I had a sexual relationship with him. He would come to me and make all kinds of sexual demands, and I submitted. My mother knew about it and allowed it to happen. I begged and pleaded with her to help me, but she said, 'You had better go along with him or we'll all be out on the street.' She told me to tell no one and to keep it a secret or the whole family would be in trouble. That was my cross to bear. Even now, I feel guilty talking to you about it. But no child should have to endure what happened to me. You must make sure that the Department of Children and Family Services does not place a child in his hands."

This woman had been my patient as a child, and she could have confided in me. I had no suspicions as she grew up. How could I know if she was telling the truth? "Did this come to you in some sort of flashback after your mother died?" I asked. She said, "No. I remember every day of it, and I will remember it all of my life." "Are you in some kind of therapy program for women who have been sexually abused as children?" I asked. She said, "No. I am not mentally ill. I know it was not my fault. I am not the one that needs therapy." "Are you willing to accuse him now and have the courts prosecute him?" I asked. She said, "No. It wouldn't serve any purpose. He would deny it all, and I couldn't prove it. It would be just like pleading with my mother to help me all over again. I am pleading with you now. Don't let him get this little girl!"

"How can you expect me to believe this? How do I know you don't have a hidden agenda and you want to hurt him for some other real or imagined reason?"

Her husband, who had not said a word, spoke up, "The story she is telling you is true. She told me about it five years ago. She wanted me to know all about it before we married. That is why we moved away after the wedding. She couldn't stand to see him, and I was afraid I might kill him."

Talk about secrets! Up until then I thought that, "Grandma drinks" and "Ralph did hard time" were family secrets.

I called the case worker at D.C.F.S. and briefly told her what information had come to me. We both agreed that under no circumstance would a child be placed in his care. The information was recorded in their computer where it will be stored indefinitely and be available to other social agencies. A letter was sent to Mr. and Mrs. King, which stated that further investigation into their application had led D.C.F.S. to come to the conclusion that they were not a suitable couple to participate in the foster child program.

I never saw or heard of the Kings again. They sold their house and moved away. What bothers me most is that the whole perverted scenario is still a secret.

SVEN'S PLACE

Dr. Desmond Morris, an animal behaviorist, wrote a book titled, *The Naked Ape*. In it he discussed man's behavior as an animal and compared it to the behavior of other animals.

He describes male dogs marking their territory with their urine. Any other dog coming into the area will know that this space belongs to "Rex" and no other dog. Presumably from smelling the urine, another dog knows a lot about "Rex" and may even challenge "Rex" for the space.

Dr. Morris says that man marks his own territory with pictures and memorabilia of himself, so that other men will know that this is "Fred's" place and know something about "Fred."

The old Swedish farmer had not been seen for several days, and his neighbors, worried about him, called the police. They found him dead in his bed. I was called to pronounce him dead as a formality. That being done, the police left and the mortician took the body to town. I was left by myself in his house. I didn't know his name or anything about him.

The walls and rooms told his life story in pictures and objects. There was a Swedish family Bible on the night-stand. It was open and appeared to have been read on a regular basis, its pages being thumbprinted and well worn. The family's marriages, births, baptisms, and deaths were dutifully recorded.

There was a picture of his mother and father, taken in Sweden, before they came to America. There were no children in the picture, and so I assumed he was born in the United States. The first picture of him and his brother was dated 1912 and showed two strapping farm boys sitting on the porch steps of this very same house. They were handsome, strong, and vital. There were several pictures taken during World War I, the war to end all wars. (How disgusted he must have been with World War II and the Korean War.) He is standing in the picture with young men just like himself, wearing a helmet and a military uniform with leggings. They are grinning and toasting the photographer with bottles of wine. I don't know if his brother ever came back. There were no more pictures of him.

He married in 1921 and there is a formal wedding picture of a stern, serious, unsmiling couple. As you follow the pictures, three children eventually appear, and his parents disappear. One child died and this was noted in a framed picture with a lock of hair.

He worked at farming. There is a photograph of him working a team of big Percherons. Later, there is a picture of him sitting on a new tractor with iron lug wheels. His pride radiates from the picture. There are pictures of assorted farm dogs, "Old Shep," and "King."

The pictures document his children growing up and that he and his wife were aging. There are class pictures from school and finally graduation photographs. Then there are pictures of married children and finally grandchildren.

Then the pictures stop. There are no new pictures of his wife or himself. She is gone. There is no one left to take his picture. He is alone. Now he too is gone.

I left the house and locked the door behind me.

Our Town's weekly newspaper wrote the obituary.

Sven Svenson

Sven Svenson, 75, died on Tuesday, April 10th at his home in Our Town. The son of Swedish immigrants, he lived and farmed in Our Town all his life. He served in the United States Army, in France, during World War I. He was a member of the V.F.W. and a lifelong member of St. Matthew's Lutheran Church. He belonged to the Scandinavian American Cultural Society. He was very active in local 4-H clubs.

Funeral services were held April 12th at St. Matthew's Lutheran Church, with interment at the Church cemetery.

He is survived by his sons, Bjorn and Gunnar; and grandchildren, Matthew, Eric, Howard and Brett.

He was preceded in death by his wife, Inga; his parents, Inar and Ingrid Svenson; his brother, Ivar; and daughter, Birgitte.

The house was sold. The first thing the new owner did was to get rid of the possessions and memorabilia of the previous owner. The house was cleaned and the walls painted. I am sure that as soon as he moved in, he began marking the territory.

BINGO

Cigarette packages are labeled with the warning that cigarette smoking is hazardous to your health. Television and radio transmit the message that it is dangerous to use drugs. How come nobody ever warned us about bingo?

Rose was hopelessly addicted to bingo. She was an eighty-year-old widow who lived alone with a little dog. Bingo was her passion. She had her cataracts fixed in order to play the game. "I can listen to talking books and play the radio, but I have got to see those numbers!" She played two or three times a week, which is pretty good for a lady who didn't drive a car and depended on others to take her to the games.

It was a blizzard! There was already a foot of snow on the ground, and it was still falling. It was also Tuesday night, which is bingo night at Saint Patrick's Church. She had to go! She made call after call to the people on her list of bingo players trying to get someone to take her to Saint Pat's. "Rose," they told her, "there is a blizzard out there." "You're just a bunch of wimps," she responded, "it's BINGO NIGHT!" The local cab driver, we had only one, refused to take her. "The hell with them," she said. She pulled on her boots and out she went with her winter coat, scarf, gloves, and cane. In her own defense she later said, "It was only three blocks."

Courage, fortitude, and motivation won out. She shook the snow from her scarf and coat and hung them on the half-empty rack. Attendance was really down, but to her it meant more chances to win.

She must have been a marvel to see; three conversations going at the same time, five bingo cards being processed, a handful of bingo chips in her right hand, and a handful of popcorn in her left. And then it happened. She swallowed a handful of chips. Bingo! She was in trouble.

The wad of chips got stuck where her esophagus goes into her stomach. The resulting severe esophageal spasm produced unbelievable chest pain. They thought she was having a heart attack, and they called the paramedics. She was too embarrassed to say anything about the bingo chips.

In the hospital emergency room she told me what had happened. A gastroenterologist was called in, and he passed a scope through her mouth and down her esophagus. Six bingo chips were retrieved.

She insisted on going home first thing in the morning. She had to feed her dog, and besides it was Wednesday, which is bingo night at Saint Michael's.

ACCOUNTING

Henry Hopkins and Jesse Stone were neighbors. Their houses and driveways were side by side on a busy street. They were both married and in their middle thirties. They had lived in Our Town all their lives. They had started kindergarten together and graduated high school together. They hated each other.

The die had probably been cast before either of them was born. Henry was born into a Christian Temperance household. They were a deeply religious conservative family. They were disciplined people who always did what was proper and principled. They believed in turning the other cheek. Henry's father was a pacifist and believed in non-violence. During World War II he had served overseas as a medic. Henry himself had been a conscientious objector during the Vietnam War. Fortunately, his number never came up. They were quiet, nonaggressive people and pretty much kept to themselves. Henry's father had held the same clerical job in Chicago for more than thirty years.

On the other hand, the Stone family was a hard-drinking, loud and boisterous group. They had no particular code or principle that the family lived by. They pretty much did whatever they wanted to do. They had no problem settling arguments among themselves or with others by fistfights. Mr. Stone had been a much decorated marine serving in the Pacific during World War II. Jesse joined the army during the Vietnam War and managed to return home unharmed. His dad had never held a continuous job for more than a few years. He had worked off and on in a variety of jobs from heavy equipment operator to over-the-road trucker.

Part of Henry's problem was his appearance. As a young child, he wore thick glasses and had a crew cut. He looked like a "nerdy" kid. Adults thought he looked cute, but the kids didn't and they teased him maliciously. He was an excellent student, which further complicated his problems. He knew the answers when the others did not, and the teachers called on him often. The other kids resented it and beat him up during recess. Turning the other cheek did not help him. The pattern continued all through grade school and high school. Academics was his only achievement. He graduated high school with honors, won a scholarship, and went away to college. It was a new life for him. He became an accountant.

In contrast, Jesse had a ball at school. He was a good-looking kid, had social skills and charisma. He became a class leader and was the leader of the pack that gave Henry such a hard time. Jesse was not much of a student, but was a moderately good athlete. He reveled in the limelight. In his junior year he got into some trouble with alcohol, drugs, and cars, but managed to con his way out of it. He was not a good enough athlete to win a college scholarship, and it was probably just as well because he really didn't want to go. When he got back from Vietnam, he got a job with a local construction company. A few years later he married and bought the house.

Henry did very well at college. He brought no old personal baggage with him to school. People who met him were meeting him for the first time and they liked what they saw. They accepted him at face value. He was the same Henry. He just didn't have to deal with confrontation. In Economics 101, he fell in love with a young woman. They were married one week after graduation and settled in Our Town. He got a good job with an accounting firm in Chicago, and three years later he bought the house. He was more than a little shocked and upset to find out that Jesse was his neighbor. He told himself, "It'll be all right. We're adults now. We were kids then." He was wrong. Leopards don't change their spots.

Jesse sat on the porch, drinking, watching Mr. and Mrs. Hopkins leave for church. "Commie bastard," he said to nobody in particular. It galled him that he had been in Vietnam while Henry was in college. He resented Henry's position and status. He resented the suit and the car and his holier-than-thou attitude. He threw the empty bottle into Henry's yard and opened another.

Every day Henry picked up the empty bottles and put them in the trash. He would go the extra mile and he would turn the other cheek. That only caused Jesse to push him further.

Jesse knew he drank too much. He stopped at the tavern every day, after work, before coming home. He often came home drunk. One night he missed the turn and ran his pickup truck across Henry's lawn, ripping ruts into the sod. On the weekend, Henry dutifully filled the ruts with black dirt and put in new sod. He still avoided confronting Jesse, and Jesse wondered just how far he could push before he got a rise out of him. The next day, driving home, Jesse wiped out Henry's mailbox as he made the turn. Henry came charging out of the house and Jesse decked him with a single punch.

The Chief of Police had known both men all their lives and knew the background. He met with both of them in Jesse's living room. Jesse had refused to go to Henry's house. "Let him come to me," he said. The chief was kind, sincere, and sympathetic. "You are grown men now. This is childish. Let bygones be bygones. You don't have to like each other, but you do have to be civil." Jesse responded as if he had been the victim. "I didn't do anything wrong. I missed the turn and hit the mailbox, and this maniac came out and attacked me. He deserved what he got." There was no making peace. The beer bottles continued to litter the lawn, and the mailbox got wiped out about once a week.

I saw Henry in the office. He was agitated, anxious, and depressed. He couldn't sleep at night because he couldn't stop thinking. He couldn't eat and was losing weight.

Worst of all, he couldn't concentrate at work. He wanted to kill Jesse. I told him, "Let the police handle it. Make a formal complaint every time he litters or damages your property. Take him to court." He shook his head. "The first time I complained to the police, my cat disappeared. The last time I complained someone threw a brick through my living room window. I personally am going to get him!" I shook my head. "Henry, it's not worth it. You'll go to jail. It's easier to sell the house and move away." "Bullshit," he said. "I'm not running away. I'm through backpedaling. I've done that all my life and it never worked. I don't have to apologize for who I am and what I am. I'm going to get him and he won't even see it coming. I won't go to jail. I have no intention of breaking the law." I wanted to medicate him to calm him down, but he refused. I asked him if he wanted to talk with a psychiatrist. He said, "No. For the first time in my life I'm responding to a threat in a positive, active way. That's good mental health." "Why did you come here today," I asked. He answered, "I just needed someone to tell this to, and you were it."

Jesse had gone on a three-day fishing trip to Wisconsin with some "Nam" buddies. While he was gone, Henry worked in his yard putting in edging around the flower beds and working on his lawn. He bought a new mailbox and post to replace his previously destroyed one. The place looked nice.

It was one o'clock in the morning and Jesse was coming home from the fishing trip. He was feeling no pain. In the light of the street lamp he saw the new mailbox. He laughed to himself and floored the accelerator. He hit the mailbox, mounted on a thick steel "I" beam set in two yards of concrete, at about fifty miles an hour. He has no recollection of being thrown through the windshield, fracturing his skull, shoulder, and several ribs. The steering wheel created havoc in his abdomen. He spent almost a month in the hospital and was unable to work for a year. He never spoke to Henry about it.

He had no insurance. He couldn't make the house payments, and the bank threatened to foreclose. The only thing he could do was sell the house and move away.

BIRDS OF A FEATHER

One of the joys of general practice, over time, is that eventually you deal only with people who like you and whom you like in return. This comes about through natural selection.

If you don't meet patients' expectations, they never come back. They also tell their friends, who have similar expectations, all about you, and, as a result, you never see them in the first place. The opposite is also true. If the patient is happy with you, he always comes back. He also tells his friends, who have similar expectations, and they eventually come under your care. This is called "word of mouth." That is how practices grow and thrive or wither and fail. I do not believe that commercial advertising helps, except perhaps to get the patient in the office the first time.

The doctor's attitude is also part of the equation. If I am unhappy with a patient, the patient will perceive it, be uncomfortable, and not come back. If I have a positive attitude with a patient, the patient is more comfortable and tends to come back. So eventually the practice is like visiting with friends.

Over time, the kind of work you do in the practice becomes defined. You keep doing more of the kinds of things you like to do, and less of the things you find unpleasant or boring.

I have never used "diet pills" as part of a weight reduction program. Up until recently, they were harmful, habit-forming, and not effective over the long term. As a result of this attitude, I had almost no one come to me for weight reduction. I am comfortable with most psychiatric patients and have been able to work with them effectively. Because of that, a large part of my practice was with emotionally disturbed people. It's almost as if there is a community network directing patients by category.

"Birds of a feather flock together." If you prescribe contraception for teenage girls, the network disseminates that information and soon there are teenage girls in your office seeking contraceptive advice. If you treat Medicaid patients in your office with kindness and consideration, they will come thirty miles to see you. Every group seems to have its own network. The biggest boon to my obstetrical practice was delivering the oldest girl in a family of five daughters. I eventually delivered babies for all of them, and for most of their friends as well.

Naomi was a lovely young woman of twenty-six who came to the clinic for the first time to get a complete history and physical exam. She was stylishly dressed, educated, and quite articulate. In response to the question, "What kind of work do you do?" she replied, "I'm a call girl." I thought I hadn't heard right, so I asked the question again and got the same answer. I was really taken back and asked, "Why do you do that?" She arched her eyebrow, laughed and said, "For the money." I did not moralize nor lecture her about her "evil ways." Instead I asked important questions about sexually transmitted diseases and how she was protecting herself and her clients. She agreed to get periodic cultures, blood tests, and smears. I tried to impress upon her the importance of condoms, but she shrugged it off as being bad for her business. (This was before AIDS.) She came to the clinic every three months for several years until she left "the life" and married. Within two weeks of first seeing Naomi, three other call girls made appointments. That year they sent me a custom Christmas card. The four of them were dressed in gay nineties costumes in an old-time saloon as "Ladies of the Night." It simply said, "Merry Christmas."

SMALL TOWN
THOUGHTS

Every country town has a place where the day begins. It's a small restaurant on Main Street, and it has been there since the town began. It's almost always called "somebody's" place; "Mom's Place," "Fritz's Place," "George's Place." They open and close in the dark. There is a menu on each table, but no one uses it. They just tell the waitress what they want. Because we are all creatures of habit, after a while, she automatically brings you what you usually order or should have ordered. Nobody complains. The food is usually delicious, especially breakfast.

Most of the interaction of the business community takes place here, over breakfast. The farmers and the doctors are usually the first people to appear. They discuss the weather and the crops and how "what's his name" is getting along. Almost always, a veterinary or political question comes up and this is chewed up along with breakfast. The bankers and the construction people come in. The group talk changes to seed money, building projects, interest rates, and the availability of money. The building contractor gives his crew instructions for today. The local police come in for coffee, one coming on duty, the other going off. It's a changing of the guard. The mayor of the town is there. This place is his information highway.

From six to seven-thirty in the morning the place is packed. On cold winter mornings the windows are frosted over, and this room feels shut off from the rest of the world. It's cozy and warm, physically and spiritually. It's like a large family having breakfast together.

Our Town used to have such a place. The building is still there, and it is still a restaurant. It is not the same. We got too big. We're not family anymore. More than half the people that live here are strangers to each other. Our Town now has three banks, a dozen contractors, sixteen police officers, ten physicians, five dentists, four optometrists, three chiropractors, and no farmers. The problem is not with what we have gained but with what we lost.

There is a myth that small towns are safe. This is not true. Small towns are small and have small populations spread out over large areas. Crime, violence, and disease can be expressed as so many cases per 100,000 people per year. If a community only has 1,000 people, it will take 100 years to have the same number of cases as a community of 100,000 people. Our Town has had its murderers and rapists. We have the wife beaters and the child abusers. We have the random violence, the car thieves, and the burglars. We have the drug addicts and the dealers. We haven't added them up for a long enough time to know that we are not safe.

I will concede that really large communities do have more problems with crime and violence than small towns. They have to deal more with crowding, poverty, and the concentration of large groups of criminally-minded people in gangs. In a large city, a Jeffrey Dahmer can be anonymous and no one knows he's there. In a small town everyone knows you and also pretty much knows what you do.

Modern transportation has brought more crime to small towns. The interstate highway system can and does deliver crime and violence to the country. Several years ago, a gang of rapists, robbers, and murderers operated along I–57. A town near Our Town had three murders in one night by a drifter, passing through. There is a town of 200 people nearby that suffered a home invasion and two people were murdered. Our Town had a home invasion and one of our lifelong residents lost his life.

There was an ongoing program on television dealing with the activities of a New York City police precinct. In each episode, the sergeant cautioned his officers with the admonition, "Be careful, it's dangerous out there."

It still is.

ADVICE

Unasked for advice is hardly ever well-received. I'm going to give it anyhow.

My advice to a physician completing a family practice residency is to go where he or she is needed. Go to a rural town where you can be all things to all people. Go where you are "The Doctor" and specialists are available at a distance.

Practice obstetrics. That is the fastest practice builder there is. First, the mother becomes your patient, then the child, then the husband, and finally, the extended family. It also pays well.

Be available to your patients. That means evening hours and being on-call. Practice medicine as a profession, not as a hobby.

Marry the right person. Your spouse is going to share this part of your life, good and bad.

Practice the best medicine, regardless of the patient's ability to pay. Be charitable to your patients. You don't have to be paid for everything you do. Patients that need to be seen, should be seen, even if they can't pay you. For one thing, they are sick. For another, they may not always be poor and you may eventually get paid. Last, but not least, they will tell the community of your compassion and dedication. Then you will have more paying patients than you can probably handle!

Become friends with your patients. Be their confidant and medical advisor. When specialized physicians are involved in complicated cases, be the captain of the ship, the conductor of the symphony.

Be there for your patients!

LAST DAY

It has been thirty years since the first day. After 180,000 patient visits and 1,500 deliveries, I'm tired.

Bob Dylan wrote and sang, "The times they are a changin'!" Change is inevitable. It is usually good and often progressive. Old-timers have trouble accepting and adjusting to change. That is why they talk so much about the good old days. I am an old-timer. It is too difficult and aggravating for me to adjust, and it's easier to just quit. Change has occurred in multiple areas, each one requiring its own adjustment.

I am sixty years old and I am tired, physically and emotionally. It is hard to listen to other people's problems when I am thinking of my own. It is getting more difficult to get up at night to respond to crisis. The burden of responsibility is getting too heavy, and I want to put it down. There are so many other things I want to do, and time is running out. There is a whole new life outside of the practice of medicine.

I don't live and practice in the country anymore. Our Town used to be a small country town. We are now the essence of suburbia. The farms are gone, replaced by subdivisions and shopping malls. A real estate article in *The Chicago Tribune* referred to Our Town as being "exclusive." The influx of new people and businesses has changed the character of our community forever.

The government and media refer to me as a "primary care health provider." It is a totally generic name implying interchangeable parts, one being as good as another. I'm sorry, but I am Barry Ladd, M.D., a family physician. There are many others similar to me, but none quite like me.

Employers and insurance companies are denying patients free choice of physicians through the financial incentives of Health Maintenance and Preferred Provider Organizations. Managed care breaks the bond between the patient and his physician. It is the bottom line that counts. Can it be done cheaper? The patient entrusts his life to the lowest bidder. Families with long-standing relationships with their physicians are being forced to switch to other clinicians who are part of the new plan. It leads to mediocrity of medical care. The patients are captive to the plan. The physician may or may not be responsive to the patients' needs. For patients who have never had a family doctor, it will make no difference because they will not know what they are missing.

I am unhappy with the medical profession. It seems to me that physicians have become too entrepreneurial. Listen to the radio and television. It's reminiscent of the old snake oil salesman selling his cure-all. The airways are full of medical commercials touting this hospital, that clinic, and that new special test. They have hired marketing people who create a need for services that were not needed before. They frighten people unnecessarily.

New family physicians coming out of residencies seem to know a lot, but don't do much. At least that's true in urban and suburban areas. They treat only the simple and routine, and refer all else to specialists. They do not do normal obstetrics, office surgery, or simple orthopedics. Perhaps they are afraid of the malpractice risk, or perhaps the patient expects or insists on being referred to a specialist. If that is true, family physicians in urban and suburban areas will disappear. They will be replaced by nurse practitioners and physician assistants who will be just as effective, and will be a whole lot cheaper.

The business of medicine has become a paper quagmire. The paperwork grows exponentially. Risk management, cost accounting, clinical justification, and appropriateness of treatment, require that physicians write down and document everything they say or do. Insurance companies have their own different forms and methodologies requiring paperwork as do hospitals, Medicare, and Medicaid. Each organization promises to reduce and minimize paperwork, but it does not happen and the pile grows.

Here we are approaching the twenty-first century and quackery still abounds. It preys on people with little hope of cure, who clutch at straws. It preys on the ignorant.

When I first came to Our Town, medical malpractice suits were almost nonexistent. Doctors made as many mistakes then as they do now. But the patients were not so quick to sue them. The doctor and patient and family had a personal relationship. The patient and family felt that, regardless of the outcome, their doctor did his best, and that was all that could be expected. All that has changed. I spent the last two weeks of my medical career in a Chicago courtroom defending a malpractice suit. (The jury found on my behalf.)

The amount of money spent unnecessarily on laboratory testing as part of defensive medicine is mind-boggling. If medical costs are to be contained, malpractice suits and awards will likewise have to be contained. One will not happen without the other.

So now what for Barry Ladd, M.D.? It's time to grow and smell the roses. It's the hope and dream of training a champion bird dog. It's playing enough golf to eventually get a hole in one. It's time with my family to make up for lost time. It's time to travel on.

Goodbye.